Praise for Piece by Piece

"Piece by Piece *is a compelling read full of lessons taught and lessons learned. With bracing candor and original humor Hauk crafts the story of an authentic life, a story of survival, resilience and hope.*

Hauk is a teacher, but also a lifelong student of people, power and perseverance. Readers will see her soul and parts of their own."

—**John Wisely**, Emmy-award winning
journalist and podcaster

"*Sheryl's willingness to share her truth—raw, painful, and unvarnished—as well as her winding path of triumph, courage and resilience is nothing short of inspiring. Her trauma and enduring strength are hers alone but her lessons are for all of us."*

—**Greg Jasperse**, Singer, Composer,
Music Educator

"*Picking up the pieces of a shattered childhood is a painstakingly slow, messy and individual process. Sheryl uses wit and humor to share her raw emotional journey and to relay that no matter how many broken pieces you may have endured, there IS a way to put them all back into a beautiful life full of love and hope for the future.*

I highly recommend this genuinely reflective and tender book."

—**Donna Schick**, Author

"Sheri's story is, at once, hopeful, heartbreaking, and engaging. I am struck by its openness and stark telling of experiences that could have produced a very different result. However, true to her nature that I've admired for years, Sheri finds her way to hope and love through her resilient and determined spirit.

As a colleague who has admired Sheri's work with students for years, I can now see why her students are drawn to her and love her deeply. I'm so grateful for her courage to share her life with us. I'm inspired by Sheri's determination to soar boldly rather than allow circumstances to anchor her in sadness or pain.

I hope that everyone who reads Sheri's story may experience healing and the courage to boldly sing their song."

—**Adam Wurst**, Music Educator,
Author '*Executive Function Skills for Teens:
How to Coach Your Teen Toward Confidence,
Independence, and Real-World Success*'

"I just finished reading and I'm honestly just so inspired. Sheryl's story is incredible and she shares it with such courage, honesty, and humor. It has left me in awe. every chapter shows just how resilient she is and her ability to turn pain into strength and something beauteous.

What struck me most is how much of the same spirit I recognized from high school. She poured that same energy into me and my artistic journey.

I feel grateful beyond words that she continued to support me on my own artistic path. and her story makes me want to keep going.

—**Danny Kornfeld**, Broadway Actor

"For as long as I can remember, one of my all-time favorite quotes is one spoken by Nelson Mandela... 'Courage is not the absence of fear but the triumph over it.'

Fast forward to one of my very favorite people, Sheryl Hauk. Her personal, painful story lives and breathes those words a million times over. The way she has so masterfully pieced together the extreme and tragic details of her life and relationships from childhood to adulthood delivers a story you don't want to stop reading.

You will laugh, you will cry and you will wish you had been there for her kicking asses and taking names. But she didn't and doesn't require that from any of us... she just needs us to hear her. Hear her story. Out of the fear and darkness... into the courage and light.

Sheryl is Triumphant! And ever always the educator, her story will teach many of us to face our own adversity and hardship and to speak up! Piece by piece, brick by brick, Lego piece by Lego piece... even if you step on one of those damn pieces in the dark."

—**Karen Newman**, Singer, Voice of
the Detroit Red Wings

Piece by Piece

A Memoir of Survival, Resilience, and the Power of Creativity

SHERYL HAUK

GLOBAL WELLNESS MEDIA
LOS ANGELES, TORONTO, MONTREAL

First Edition. Published by:
Global Wellness Media
Stratedgy LLC
440 N Barranca Ave #2027
Covina, California, 91723
(866) 467-9090
GlobalWellnessMedia.com

Publisher's Note: The views expressed in this work are solely those of the authors and do not necessarily reflect the views of the publisher, and the publisher hereby disclaims any responsibilities for them.

Editor: Bobbie Walton, Eric D. Groleau

Piece by Piece/ Sheryl Hauk. — 1st ed.
ISBN: 978-1-957343-31-0 (Paperback)
ISBN: 978-1-957343-37-2 (Hardcover)
ISBN: 978-1-957343-33-4 (ePub)

Dedicated to my Grandchildren and all survivors

May you always know your worth, trust your voice, and build boldly with the pieces you're given.

From Me to You

I didn't write this book to be inspirational.
I wrote it because the truth matters.

For most of my life, I was told not to talk. Not to tell. Not to write anything down.

So, I stopped.

But silence has a cost, and I've paid it.
In pain.
In health.
In years.

This book is me breaking that silence.

I've tried to tell the truth the way I lived it: in layers, in fragments, with detours and side stories, with moments of hard-won humor.

Some chapters might make you laugh.
Others may stop your breath.

That's how survival works—it doesn't follow a script. It follows the path you carve through the dark.
This story begins in darkness because that's where survival starts.
If it feels heavy at first, keep reading. There is light. There is music. There are dogs.

The feelings, the events, the memories?
They're mine.
I didn't embellish them.
I didn't soften them.
I didn't try to turn them into something they weren't.
I lived them.
I am still living them.

If you're holding this book and you've ever been silenced—by fear, by shame, by someone else's power—I hope you find something in these pages that helps you claim your own pieces. Not every story needs to be shared publicly. But every story deserves to be honored and heard, including yours.

We don't get to choose all the pieces.
But we do get to choose what we build.
Still building,

Sheryl

Sheryl at 2 years old

Table of Contents

Measure 3 – Truth and Turning Points

Measure 4 – Legacy, Voice, and Meaning

Prologue
Writing Things Down

I was a music teacher for over forty years. The kind who kept cheese sticks in her office, spare bow ties in her purse, and broken-hearted teenagers in tune, at least most of the time. I taught music but, really, I taught survival. How to breathe through a panic attack during a solo. How to stand tall when the world keeps folding you in half. How to hold a note—and your dignity—when everything else is falling apart.

When I was younger, I wrote in a diary. It had a lock, you know, those little pretend locks—the ones parents can easily break. My lock was broken by the person I was supposed to trust the most and trusted the least—My Father.

There's a lot to say about him, but first, the diary.

That diary was my one place to talk when I couldn't confide in anyone else. The last time I wrote in it was during my senior year of high school. He found it again. This time, he was furious. He hit me. He smothered my face with a pillow so I couldn't breathe. Then he punished everyone around me, just for being there.

The lesson? Don't write anything down.
And yet…Here I am.
Writing something down.

It's been over forty years since that moment, and, since then, all my thoughts, fears, and light have lived in my head.

So here I am now. Over 60. A retired music teacher, director, mother, grandmother, sister, friend, wife, and… SURVIVOR.

Describe me? I'm the most conservative liberal who's ever lived. Yes, we do exist. I have been married for a very long time, with four grown children, four grandchildren, and one more on the way. I live in the suburbs and cook dinner for my Husband every night. I silently pray for the ones I love and for the world.

What finally made me sit down and type?
I fell.
Flat on my face.

For someone clinging to the idea that, at a mature age, one can still be attractive, eating pavement is downright horrifying.

Two black eyes, cuts across my face and forehead, and a swollen knee like a round ripe fruit no one wants to eat. I didn't leave the house for weeks. I described myself as Frankenstein's bride, although she looked better in James Whalen's version of Mary Shelley's character. And that wasn't even the big scare. It started with a routine X-ray, which led to a CT scan. Nodules—dozens of them. Something called 'ground glass.' A radiologist glanced at the images, muttering that he wasn't convinced it wasn't a "fast-growing lung cancer."

Fear has a way of scrambling the pieces of your life. So I did what I've always done when the picture made no sense.

I gathered the mismatched pieces—broken ones, discolored ones, odd ones—and snapped them together into something new. Something creative. Something better.

Which is exactly why I chose the title **Piece by Piece**— because I've spent my life snapping pieces together. So maybe writing this is finally the project I've been designing in my head for years.

That week nearly shattered me.
But it didn't.
Because now I get to tell the story.

Now I get to write.

Measure 1
Triage and Thresholds

Chapter 1
The Little Room

In 2003, I thought I was finally going to breathe a sigh of relief, and I mean, finally. I had a 'real job,' with medical insurance, a retirement plan, and a wardrobe—both in my closet and in the school costume collection I was bequeathed.

My firstborn was graduating high school with honors and about to receive the National Scholastic Gold Key at the Kennedy Center in Washington, D.C. for her art portfolio. My second child, first son, was simply and chaotically surviving high school and hockey. Not me, I'm a survivor, but I never survived being the Goalie Mom. My youngest, the one who screamed anytime I left him with a friend to work at the co-op preschool—boy, that was fun—was finishing kindergarten. And Kai—my beautiful, brilliant, curious Kai was going in for a routine tonsillectomy.

Maybe it wasn't a breath of relief, but life was somewhat 'normalizing' in my head.

Being the multitasker I am, I sat in the hospital waiting room with a pen in one hand and a stack of graduation announcements in the other. Everything felt like it was landing where it should, and then it all unraveled, again.

My Husband had disappeared, probably to get a cup of coffee—coffee deserves its own book at our house—or check out the long, unknown hospital corridors to nowhere. A new adventure—the kind he loves.

Sitting alone, ready to tackle handwritten, addressed graduation invitations, I was starting to let myself think, believe, feel, "Maybe…maybe this time we're okay." Then the doctor walked out.

White as a ghost. Eyes darting. Voice low. He asked me to come into "the little room." NEVER trust the little room. This was not a tonsil problem.

The doctor didn't know exactly what it was yet, despite considering himself brilliant. In fact, he did praise himself—yes, praised himself—for not cutting "a very vascular mass" two minutes into a routine tonsillectomy. He said if he'd cut it, Kai could have bled to death on the table.

Oh—and by the way—this thing? This giant tumor? He was supposed to catch it in his office by looking IN my son's nose. But as a pediatric ear, nose, and throat (ENT) doctor, apparently "looking carefully" wasn't on his to-do list the day Kai was brought in to see the 'specialist' for multiple and prolonged stuffy, bloody noses.

To tell the truth, I was too stunned, too deep in survival mode, when the doctor called to give us "referrals to specialists." Wasn't he the specialist? And, over the phone? To top it off, he wished me a cheery, "Good luck."

GOOD LUCK?

I didn't even have the energy to think, "*You misdiagnosed him, and maybe you should be paying for all the surgeries, the counseling, the stolen possibilities.*" Not to mention the LEGO kits.

An emergency CT scan soon revealed the diagnosis: Juvenile Nasal Angiofibroma (JNA).

It was a rare, benign tumor that filled my son's skull. It started in his nasal cavity, pushed through the bones, wrapped around both optic nerves and the carotid artery. It destroyed the base of his skull and punched through the dura—the protective membrane around the brain—squashing his temporal lobe like a sponge.

This was my child. My child. My baby.

The world didn't stop. Not for a second.

This was the first year of my return to teaching full-time. The classes included middle school choir and music appreciation. I welcomed all the kids no one knew what else to do with.

I was driving thirty minutes between my school, three of my kids' schools, hockey, soccer, piano lessons, going to graduate school, cooking, cleaning, homework, and even mowing the lawn. You get the idea. I was a little busy, like the rest of the over-achieving 'extended' baby-boomer women.

Somewhere in between, I was meeting with doctors—plural, doctors—from the University of Michigan Hospital Skull Base Clinic and watching my eight-year-old's face grow paler by the day.

And still, the world kept turning. People still expected me to show up. Smile. Function. Participate.

My oldest was being celebrated—a big moment. Graduation, honors, all eyes on her. It was supposed to be HER moment. Instead, family flew in from all directions, even the in-laws—the 'other side'—to witness both Kai's surgery and my daughter's graduation. They weren't worried about him; they came because it was an event—something to be part of. My mother-in-law cried, primarily, I suspect, because of how hard it was for her.

My sister showed up at the hospital with a camera and a mission. She handed me the camera, posed beside Kai, and smiled, while my fragile son lay unconscious— head completely wrapped, jaw broken, just two hours out of a 21-hour surgery. Six surgeons had opened his skull to remove a massive tumor. She needed that picture—proof, I guess, that she was there.

In short, everyone had something to say, something to make themselves feel involved in what was happening, something for each of them to feel important about.

I was determined not to let the noise of other people's self-importance drown out what really mattered. My mission: helping Kai survive and, maybe, just maybe, thrive. That's what moms do. That's what survivors do.

I knew what it looked like from the outside—if anyone had bothered to look, which most didn't. Just a family juggling milestones. This was not a juggling act. This was triage. Every moment I wasn't focused on my son felt like a betrayal. Not to anyone else. To him.

From the outside, it might have looked organized, as if we had a system. Inside, it was like a giant mess of snap-together pieces spilled across the floor. No instructions. No picture on the box. Just broken pieces everywhere and no idea where to start.

So I did what I always did: I showed up. I hosted a graduation party. I held bloody noses. I taught school. I hired my own sub. I fielded questions from surgeons.

And Kai? He kept building LEGO kits.

I kept placing them on the shelves in his bedroom. Tiny pieces. One snap at a time. Because building with LEGO blocks made sense—when nothing else did.

The world didn't pause.
Neither did I.
Not because I was strong.
Because I had no choice.

Chapter 2
Hypervigilance
(And Monte Carlo)

"How do you look so normal after all you've survived?" people ask. Believe me, there's plenty behind that question—especially moments like when my son's ENT doctor wished me, "Good luck!" after discovering a softball-sized tumor in his skull—yes, softball, not baseball.

Trauma doesn't simply disappear—it reshapes itself. My childhood left me plenty of unexpected 'gifts,' not least of which is a constant state of hypervigilance.

"Hypervigilance is defined as a state of extreme alertness and watchfulness, often bordering on heightened awareness of potential threats or dangers. It's characterized by being constantly on guard, even when there's little actual risk." The Google definition is much longer, but you get the idea.

I can always sense when things aren't right—even the stuff I am not supposed to hear or see. I feel tension in a room before anyone else notices.

Sometimes that's useful. Sometimes it's not.

You hear things not meant for your ears. You see things others try to hide that you would rather not see. Sometimes, it makes people think you're *pupule*.

Pupule is the *Hawai'ian* word for crazy. Did I mention I grew up in *Hawai'i*? Yes, I can be a "little *pupule*"—can't we all?

Like the time I jumped off a 50-foot bridge. Or the time I flew to *Hawai'i* on Wednesday, testified and flew out Thursday in order to be back to teach on Friday. Not from California but from Michigan— ten hours away.

There are also hundreds of times when my teaching methods were a little different—trust me. I once got a gift from three graduating students, a conducting baton, in a wooden case, inscribed, "There is a method behind her madness." Are you convinced?

Case in point: Why I'm Not a Cruise Line VIP

Not long ago, my mother begged me to accompany her on a cruise to the French Riviera. The thought of going on yet another cruise with my MOTHER was *pupule*. I said YES?

Truth be told, I wasn't signing up for another mother-daughter cruise; I was signing up for a chance to knock off a couple of bucket-list items.

I set two personal objectives before we left port:
1. Wander among the ruins of Rome.
2. Play the roulette wheel at Monte Carlo's Royal Casino—my one reliable winning game.

Goal #1: I booked a Vespa ride for my 87-year-old mother and me. She donned the helmet and slid into the sidecar. I climbed on behind the Roman teenager who was driving and whispered, "My mom likes to go fast."

And fast we went. With her giggling, we tore through the streets of Rome, saw the ruins, and topped the evening off with a little gelato. Did I mention she requested to sit behind the young Roman, instead of in the sidecar, and finally won? She rode on the back, holding onto the eighteen-year-old, all the way to the Basilica in Vatican City.

Mission #1—Accomplished.

Goal #2: Our little sail yacht couldn't dock in Monte Carlo as planned. The captain attributed the issue to the weather, but all the other, larger, and more expensive boats didn't have a problem. A better explanation: The Monte Carlo Grand Prix was in full swing, and every trillionaire had already claimed the harbor. No room at the inn.

Instead of docking in Monte Carlo, we ended up four train stops away—in a town whose name still trips me up: Cagnes-sur-Mer. I can't say it right yet, but I'm not giving up.

I woke early, dressed in my 'French Best,' and dragged my mother off the boat in her clothes of choice; capris and a fanny pack. Nothing screams 'American Tourist' more to Monte Carlo—one of the many challenges of traveling with my mother.

I dutifully followed her off the crowded train to the Hop-on-Hop-off bus. She was thrilled—her favorite way to visit a city. Although, I bet if there were a Vespa to rent, she might have gone that route.

Finally, we hopped off at the square in front of the Royal Casino. To get inside—and yes, it included a gift shop—we had to go through security. I must've passed the Monte Carlo 'what-to-wear' checklist, because they didn't check my bag and waved me through with a respectful nod. My mother? That was another story. They thoroughly searched her fanny pack. Must've been the capris.

The doors for the actual gambling hall did not open until 2 p.m. BUT I had thought ahead, joined the club, and was going to be allowed to enter at 1 p.m. However, like everything capris, the door 'sentry' took one look at my mother—in her fanny pack and capris—and turned us away.

With a couple that my mother had befriended on the cruise—latched onto is a better description—we had made it through the Hop-on-Hop-off bus tour and even lunch. According to my mother, lunch was too expensive for her taste. Who orders only soup and water at the Café de Paris? And smoking patrons? How dare the French do that.

By 1:45 p.m., it was time for Goal #2—roulette. But now, she said her legs hurt. She was tired. This was classic. Just like Amsterdam. There, she demanded a wheelchair, only to find out she might miss her flight because KLM was waiting for other passengers who needed assistance. She leaped off that van, sprinted through the airport with her carry-on in tow, cut to the front of the customs line, raced down ten gates, and made that flight.

Sure—now her legs hurt. Now she wanted a wheelchair. She made a big show of saying she'd head back to the boat alone—probably because her 'friends' had already disappeared toward the slot machines. Then she leaned in and whispered, "If I don't get lost." UGH. No roulette table for me.

Mission #2—Not so much accomplished.

We ran to the platform—my mother never walks—just as a train pulled in, headed to Cannes. Yes, the exact direction we were supposed to go.

But my mother stopped under the list of destinations and announced we were on the wrong platform. Unbelievable, Mom.

My Husband proudly tells people I can remember every street I've ever been on—thanks to that lovely hypervigilance. He even claims I can find every Target in North America.

BUT this time? According to her, I was wrong. I ran to catch the train, but the doors wouldn't open—because the loud lady in the capris wasn't getting on that train. And apparently, this time…capris trumped my intuition.

A long, long ten minutes later, a new train arrived. Without thinking, I jumped up and yelled to my mom, "This is the right train!" Unintentionally forgetting to purchase tickets, we boarded. UGH again. We found seats facing the double doors. A man—maybe in his twenties—got on behind us carrying a strange black bag. He dropped it and moved to the other side of the train car. Then he started to walk away.

OH NOOOOO… I'm an American. And while most of us—*not me*—dress like tourists, we all know one thing: You *never* leave your bag unattended. Not for a bathroom break. Not for a croissant. Not for a second.   We've been told a thousand times in every airport: No bag gets left behind.

"HE IS NOT LEAVING HIS BAG!"

Every part of me screamed. And yes, eventually, I stopped pretending it was just in my head. I locked eyes with him and said, "You're not leaving that bag." He glanced down the train, as if looking for someone to help him. I kept shaking my head—over and over and over "Not today," I said. "No, not today. Not today." I was really thinking, "I am not dying today on a train with my mother in capris."

He picked up the bag, dropped it where he was standing, and then moved to the other side of the cabin. Once again, he kept inching away from the bag. Farther and farther, looking at someone in the next train. His breathing quickened. He was clearly in distress. I know that look.

After 40 years of teaching teenagers, I've seen it a thousand times. That same face they make when they swear they turned in their homework—and absolutely did not.

I stood up and blocked his path. That's the crazy in me. He was NOT going to do this, and I was not going to let him— all the while, everyone looking at me like I was out of my mind. "You're not leaving that bag," I said louder, in English. He answered in French. Of course, I had no idea what he said. Wish I'd studied a little French.

Ironically, my mother didn't offer a translation— even though she took French in high school and spent the last cruise pretending she understood every word.

He was startled that an older—*though I like to think I look younger*—English-speaking woman, dressed in the latest French fashion—yes, an American—would dare to challenge him.

But why wouldn't I? I'm a Daughter of the American Revolution. I'm not in the club, but—trust me—I've got the pedigree. I'm a direct descendant from Chase, as in Samuel Chase, Founding Father, signer of the Declaration of Independence; Alexander Parris, as in Parris Island, the Marine Base for basic training; and Smith, as in John Smith and Pocahontas...no, not Pocahontas.

By now, everyone knew what I was thinking, including the British man sitting across from me and the Muslim family of three generations comforting each other—unsure whether the problem was the loud American or the man with the black bag.

However, probably not my mother.

I insisted we get off at the next stop. She announced—loud enough for the entire car to hear—that I was imagining things. She really was thinking I was *pupule*—it does run in my family.

I yelled, "Fine. I'm imagining it. We are getting off the train." She wouldn't budge. She had 'God' on her side. The train door wouldn't open.

A ticket taker—train official—started asking for tickets in the next car. CRAP. Between a man I need to stare down so we don't all die, and having to take care of this ticket thing, it might just be too much. Of course, everyone else is thinking, "Crazy American woman making a scene because she has no ticket." Nothing money can't fix, right? RIGHT!

"50 euros," the ticket taker said in broken English. Not the €9 it was supposed to cost? UGH AGAIN. I handed him €50 in cash. No—he corrected himself—"50 *each*." Each? Double UGH!

My mother tried to find cash in her fanny pack but had none because she had been scammed by the Roman taxi driver outside the Vatican Museum four days earlier. How convenient she hadn't replaced it during a trip she was going to pay for—just saying.

Back to the train. I fumbled with my wallet again, looking for my credit card, still keeping an eye on the guy with the bag or, without the bag, as he still did not claim it. Another train official appeared and stood behind the man with—or without—the black bag across the aisle from where he stood.

Now the black-bag man was breathing even harder. I mean, visibly through his mouth, making grunting noises. He was also trapped between train officials. They asked him for his ID and this crazy English-speaking AMERICAN woman kept demanding he not leave his black bag and walk away. "It will be all right," I heard coming from everywhere: the British man, the train official, even the Muslim grandma sitting across from me.

Strangely enough, nothing from my mother. For a moment, I thought maybe she trusted my instinct, my hypervigilance, for once. It would make sense because she was the only one on the train who knew how I had become so hypervigilant—how pain and hurt made me pay attention to survive.

Again, in true mom fashion, she acted like nothing was happening. She leaned in and said, "I have to go to the bathroom. I mean, I *really* need to go." What is another term for UGH—because how many times is that?

Eventually—two minutes or an hour later, I honestly couldn't tell—we reached the little village where our sailing yacht was docked, waiting for us to return. Though probably not eagerly. She needed to find a bathroom! The train official manually opened the door for my mother and me. She ran off to find a bathroom.

I breathed a sigh of relief—we were finally off the train. As my mother bolted into the village—we all know why, and it wasn't to escape a potential explosion—I turned around to look. The train didn't move. No other doors opened. No other passengers walked off.

A train official stuck his head out a small crack in the open door. "OK. Everything OK!" he yelled in his French accent. The door closed. The train left. I chased my mother away from the platform.

After a bit of stress-shopping in the village—and finally finding a bathroom in the local bar—we made our way back to the sailboat.

That evening, the other passengers were swapping stories. They'd been stuck in Monte Carlo for over an hour because the trains were delayed. No one knew why. I didn't either—not officially, anyway.

Later that night, as the yacht hoisted her sails toward the next port, word came through: A second suspicious black bag had been found on the tracks. Trains—plural—between Monte Carlo and Cannes had been halted. It was the week of the Grand Prix and the Cannes Film Festival.

Perfect timing for disaster.

Perfect timing for a trauma survivor to make everyone listen.

I realized something that day: Hypervigilance isn't some flaw in my wiring. It's the alarm system I built—because I had to. I learned to scan for danger the way other kids learned to tie their shoes. To spot the cracks before the whole thing crumbles. To pull out the loose pieces before someone gets buried.

It's exhausting.
It's not normal.

But it's what My Father taught me.
Not through lessons, but through survival.

It's what made me notice.
And maybe—just maybe—that was enough.

Chapter 3
Broken by Design

I didn't always understand hypervigilance. You know, when you see something you're not supposed to see—like men quietly leaving black bags at the edge of a train platform—you try to brush it off. But your heart's already racing. Your palms are sweating. You're already calculating exits, escape routes, and worst-case scenarios.

That's what it's like. Except, it doesn't turn off. It didn't start on that train. It started in my childhood home. A long time ago. Simply put—not so simple—I am a survivor of childhood abuse.

I don't like to compare my abuse with anyone else's. Trauma is trauma—whether it happened once or over and over again.

For me to judge, compare, or negate anyone's experience is not to listen.

Not to understand.

Not to be empathetic.

Not to be what I believe is human.

That said—and I mean this only to provide context—I've had more than one mental-health professional tell me they'd never heard a childhood story as horrific as mine.

Love to hear that.

It makes me feel a whole lot better.

NOT.

Probably says more about the circles they travel in—or the millions who don't have a voice. Believe me, my journey hasn't exactly been *Clair de Lune*—more like *O Fortuna* from *Carmina Burana*.

If my childhood was a stage, My Father wrote the script, directed the scene, and made sure no one heard me scream. He was supposed to protect me. Love me. Keep me safe. Instead, before I was even born, he decided I would be:

His project.
His property.
His possession.

That translated to abuse:
Physical abuse
Psychological abuse
Sexual abuse

Planned
Controlled
Systematic
Strategic
Disciplined
Intentional

I dreamed of a dad who'd scare off monsters. Instead, I learned how to fight them alone.

He was trained for it. The United States Naval Academy taught him how to dominate, control, and break people down. Putting incoming plebes—young men, not women at the time— through mental and physical conditioning.

Years later, John McCain wrote in his biography—yes, that John McCain; Navy pilot, Vietnam POW, United States Senator—that he survived torture in Hanoi because of the brutal training he'd received as a plebe at Annapolis.

The upperclassman assigned to him? My Father—the same man who planned my abuse before I was even born—taught other men how to survive captivity.

But me?

I was the captive in my own childhood.

This man 'raised' me:
Not to be a daughter
To be a project
A possession
A controlled environment

There are four trauma responses: fight, flight, freeze, and fawn. We don't willingly choose—the back of the brain does. I'm a fighter. That comes with its pros and cons.

If you've known me for more than a hot minute, you probably know this, I'm not always the loudest in the room—but I speak up when something's wrong. I might hold back…until I don't. "If you're mine, you get the whole heart." No half measures. That was a Facebook Nametests meme, but it might as well be my personal motto. I'll carry your pain like it's mine—and maybe rearrange the seating chart while I'm at it.

People tend to have strong opinions about me. Love or hate—there's not much in between. I've made peace with that. Mostly.

I've been called intense. Too much. Overprotective. But if you'd survived what I have, you'd understand.

I don't miss much. I don't let things slide—especially when kids or survivors are at risk. You can bring snacks to a subdivision meeting. I'll bring justice, trauma-informed awareness, and a sensible choir arrangement.

Maybe it's karma.

Perhaps it's God.

Maybe it's just that I'm a Leo born in the Year of the Tiger.

Honestly? If My Father had read my birth chart, he might've picked a different project.

I learned quickly. But I never bowed to the abuse. I didn't give in. I fought back—not just with screams—with intellect, defiance, and a refusal to be owned. I resisted his control, recoiled from his touch, and challenged his twisted plans for me with arguments no child should've had to make. He might've had power over my body, but he never got my mind. Not once. Not ever. And I paid the price. I was beaten. Smothered. Denied the kind of parental love every child deserves. Worse, he tried to convince me that what he gave me was love—that it was special.

WTF?

As a child, I spoke up.

I told my friend—that wasn't fair, she was a kid too!

I told the adult at the Children's Evangelical Bible Club Teacher Training.

I told my mother's friend—a school counselor?

I told my youth pastor—what did he care?

I told a schoolteacher.

Adults didn't listen or take action. They did nada. Zip. Zilch. They nodded, clucked, handed me a Bible verse—or worse, suggested I "pray about it." The least I can say is they looked the other way.

The truth is, most of them turned their heads so fast they probably needed a chiropractor. I stopped expecting help and started looking for something else—something that made sense of cruelty, silence, and survival.

My mother was a voracious reader. She'd get so absorbed in a book; she'd ignore me completely—even if I was shouting a question five inches from her face.

Maybe that's why I hated to read—except Holocaust stories. I devoured such books as *Mila 18, The Diary of Anne Frank,* and *The Third Reich,* with a relentless, almost frantic curiosity. One of the only truly wise things my mother ever said was that my fixation made sense. She said I could relate to the injustice, the cruelty, and the deafening silence of people who should've spoken up but didn't. She wasn't wrong.

But the kind of cruelty My Father inflicted?
It doesn't just silence you.
It breaks something.
Everything.

It takes the LEGO brick projects—those carefully built, hard-won spaces of beauty, safety, and healing—and shatters them with one careless sweep.

The worst part? No one sees it happen.
If you name it, they call you the problem.
I know what I'm feeling when it happens.
I know why it cuts so deep—because I was strong enough to survive my past.

I'm not broken.
Just rebuilt—with different pieces.

I'm a SURVIVOR.

Chapter 4
Lights Up

My husband and sons dragged me next door to try a virtual reality (VR) simulation—something terrifying: Jumping off the Sears Tower.

They were certain I'd freeze.
I didn't. I closed my eyes and jumped.
"How did you do that so fast?" they asked.
I shrugged. "I do it every day."
They laughed.
I didn't.

Because jumping—into fear, into risk, into what comes next—is something I've done my whole life.

That's what people don't see. People see me smiling on stage. Confident. Collected. Baton in hand.

What they don't see is what it takes to get there. A new gown from Macy's—because really, who doesn't need a new black gown? A concert program edited at least a hundred times—because I still can't spell. Narration printed in a font big enough for me to actually read.

What they *really* don't see is the hypervigilance. You know what that means now. The sheer will it takes to stand in front of hundreds of teenagers and ask them to trust me with their voices.

That's exactly what my family tried to do with the jump simulation. They dared me to try. I did. No hesitation. I jumped. I do it every day.

I closed my eyes and jumped out of teaching and into retirement. Theoretically, this is supposed to be the 'afterlife'—the part where you rest, travel, and finally bring those cortisol levels down.

I traveled back to my childhood home of *Hawai'i*, where I rented an extraordinarily expensive apartment with a view of Diamond Head. One eighth the size of my home; four times my mortgage. Nice, right? Wrong.

I was attempting the impossible; help my homeless, bi-polar, emotionally explosive brother 'transition back into society.' Instead of sipping a Mai Tai on the 7th floor lanai, I became a regular at every psych ward. I think we hit them all and developed 'first-name relationships' with the staff. Some got guava cake. Some got a dose of tiger sista. They never knew which one was coming.

At the Honolulu First District Court, I mastered two things; getting through security without taking off my shoes and locking eyes with a judge until justice blinked first.

The apartment *was* lovely—until my brother moved in for exactly one day and started throwing away my things, **especially** the *Elle* magazine featuring one of my famous alumni—Ryan Destiny. Heartbreaking!

Then my mother showed up. YAY!? She was on vacation with her friend—I repeat, on VACATION—not in *Hawai'i* to help me or my brother.

The best part came when My Father called me for the first time directly in years to tell me he "cared for me and loved me," but to get off his island "NOW!" A little stressed? Really?

I was now dreaming of waking up at 4 a.m.—shoveling snow just to get the car out of the driveway, fixing the copy machine five times before 6 a.m., greeting sleepy kids, and warming up our singing voices to "I Love my mom-my," every day by 7:15 a.m.—Monday through Friday. I MISS WORK!

So, when I was invited to act as the interim director at a local community choir—just one concert, four rehearsals—I closed my eyes and jumped once again.

One night a week. One hundred and twenty adults. "No auditions, just joy." That's what they told me. And, for a minute, I believed them.

I walked into the first rehearsal with a cautious heart and open arms. The singers were lovely, warm, eager, and ready to sing as loudly as they could, regardless of whether the pitch matched the music on the page.

The repertoire—list of songs, for you newbies—chosen by the previous director might have worked well for a small glee club in a high-school-cafeteria musical. Unfortunately, we were neither small, nor gleeful, nor in a cafeteria. The music left the choir underprepared and me wondering if I'd accidentally walked into a casting call for *Glee: The Budget Cuts Edition*.

I thanked the eclectic group of singers for letting me be part of their musical journey, then added a little joke, "I got to put on makeup today!"

I explained I'd taken a terrible fall, and this was the first time since then I'd been able to get dressed up. They laughed. Just like that, we began to build the connection that's essential to making music together.

I took a breath. And then...the whispers started. The side-eyes. The quiet power plays. Some singers said one thing to my face and another behind closed doors. Not all of them, but enough to notice.

It became clear that not everyone was comfortable with someone like me—a director with opinions, experience, and, God forbid, expectations. I didn't demand praise. I asked—no, needed—to be treated with respect and professionalism. I asked for clarity. For collaboration.

Let me be clear, I wasn't asking to be worshiped. I just wanted people to talk to me face-to-face instead of around me. That hypervigilance has heard it already.

I've spent my life building musical communities where people felt safe enough to be vulnerable. And in order to sing— really sing—people have to feel safe. I've experienced what happens when that kind of environment exists—visit Apple Music and type Sheryl Hauk/Laker Express.

I've seen, no, heard what happens when all—singers, accompanist, and director—feel safe. This? This was not that.

Strangely enough. The concert theme was *We Are One: Songs of Love, Hope, and Unity.* It was politics, sure—but the kind that wore black dresses and smiled through applause.

The performance went well, considering there were only four rehearsals together. The audience clapped. Many smiled. A few cried—hopefully from happiness. I was presented with the most beautiful bouquet I'd ever been gifted. A tenor joyously exclaimed he couldn't wait until next season. I even smiled— genuinely—as I walked offstage.

Yet, it wasn't long before I felt the air hang, dense, like something true and unspoken sitting in the back row. In the afterlife—the place where I was supposed to find peace—I found more of the same broken behaviors I'd worked so hard to leave behind.

The reality is; when you've survived real trauma, you don't have the energy for petty cruelty anymore. You don't have the appetite for fake smiles and passive-aggressive agendas.

I had offered something beautiful, something real. I also left that season knowing this. I won't—can't—walk into another room like that unless I'm seen. Heard. Respected. Like the professional human being I am.

They say retirement is the afterlife.
For me, it felt like another test.
But this time, I passed it.
On my terms.

Chapter 5
Spiral Wisdom

I've had many counselors. Men, women, doctors, social workers, mystics, etc. But one—the most recent—well, she wasn't even supposed to be my guru.

We met by accident, or maybe by fate. It started with a fundraiser for teachers in the district where I'd worked for years as the high school Choral Director and Fine Arts Coordinator.

My classroom occasionally benefited from a few awarded scholarships. It had the plaque glued to the door to prove it. Strange, I always seemed to be more on the giving end. Not a complaint. Just one of those curious little imbalances that no one talks about, like an inside joke with the universe.

Still, there we were—raffle tickets, baskets of donated goods, and that slightly desperate energy from staff trying to look grateful while discreetly eyeing the basket full of Lions football paraphernalia, complete with a bottle of vodka sporting a roaring Lion on the label.

I had a lot of raffle tickets. A perk of being a 'sponsor.' Nothing really tempted me; not the Lions basket, not the "Mommy Spa Days," not even the stack of gift certificates to nail salons where your feet soak in fish tanks.

But there was one empty jar. I love to 'win.' The odds were definitely in my favor. I stuffed every last ticket in there. It was practically begging me to do that. Bonus, the jar was labeled Wisdom. Wisdom? Yes, please. I could use a double helping— maybe with a side of clarity and a chaser of peace.

One by one, I stuffed every last ticket into that empty jar like I was investing in a scratch-off retirement plan. Surprise. I won! My prize? A free session with a counselor who, as it turned out, was also a psychotherapist, a medium, and a licensed professional who took insurance. A three-for-one deal—and by far the most useful raffle I've ever won.

Her office was filled with glowing crystals, Himalayan salt lamps, and the scent of something between eucalyptus and 'grounding energy.' But it wasn't the rocks, the oils, or even the fact that she talked to dead people. It was her insight. Her steadiness. Her lack of judgment. She was exactly what I needed. Two 'mature' women, saving the world—one therapeutic download at a time.

She introduced me to PACE. No, not 'pace yourself'— although that advice would've come in handy, too. Not Pace, my former boss—one of the more impressively incompetent administrators of my career. PACE: Positive and Adverse Childhood Experiences.

PACE is the updated, more balanced version of ACE, which only tracked the horror. It tries to account for both sides of childhood; what hurt you and what helped.

The positive side isn't empty.
Not by a long shot.

I've had a purpose.
Connection.
Music.

Students who are still in my life—sharing movie premiere, Broadway opening, book launch, wedding, or baby shower.

I brought my own truth, decades of teaching, of building something real. I was a quarterfinalist for the Grammy Teacher of the Year award. Nominee for Life Changer of the Year. Recipient of MSVMA Lifetime Emeritus Award. And even finalist for *Hawai'i* 1980 Junior Miss Pageant!

But the other side—the adverse part—is a pain in the *'ōkole*—Hawai'ian for rear end, in case you're wondering. That part doesn't just haunt the past. It *lives* in my body. It shows up in the CT scans, in the 190 heartbeats per minute, and in the dark blue hue of my fingers when cortisol floods my system.

According to my counselor, and a whole stack of research published in journals I now recognize by acronym, childhood trauma like mine doesn't just hurt—it reshapes the body.

Severe trauma doesn't just shorten life.

It accelerates cellular aging.

It raises the risk for heart disease, stroke, autoimmune disorders, lung cancer, and a lovely cocktail of mental health diagnoses.

Now there's even a tool to help. It's a simple list. Ten adverse experiences:

- physical abuse
- emotional abuse
- sexual abuse
- physical neglect
- emotional neglect
- domestic violence
- household substance abuse
- mental illness in the home
- incarcerated parent
- divorce

And ten protective ones:

- unconditional love
- a best friend
- belonging to a group
- a trusted non-parent adult
- opportunities for fun
- feeling safe at home

- a predictable routine
- a good school environment
- being affirmed for your strengths
- being supported during hard times

You circle what applied to your childhood. That's it. No disclaimer. No counselor standing by.

It's used in healthcare now to qualify people for coverage of all the outstanding outcomes noted. The reality? It doesn't matter how many dance classes I take, how many health food kits I buy, or that I don't smoke, and I live 'clean.'

Sometimes, you just get abused.
From birth.
Planned.
Like me.

According to my doctors—and backed by landmark research published in the Journal of the American Medical Association (JAMA)—the numbers only get more terrifying when you dig into the details:

- A CDC–Kaiser Permanente study found that people with six or more ACEs die, on average, 20 years earlier than those with none.
- Four or more ACEs double or triple the risk of early death from heart disease, stroke, and cancer.
- Survivors of trauma face:
  - 2.7 times greater risk of being diagnosed with ischemic heart disease
  - 1.9 times greater risk of stroke
  - 3 to 4 times increased odds of developing lung cancer and autoimmune disease
- Severe early trauma accelerates 'epigenetic aging'—adding a decade or more to your biological clock.

- Nearly 1 in 3 cases of adult depression, anxiety, PTSD, bipolar disorder, and substance abuse can be traced back to ACEs.
- Survivors carry a 10–25-year reduction in life expectancy tied specifically to chronic mental illness.

It's horrifying—and it 's real. UNNECESSARY, I might add.

I asked my doctor, "So…does that mean my time is soon up?" She hesitated. Then answered carefully, "The statistics don't tell the whole story.

Some survivors don't survive. Not really. Some die quickly—suicide, overdose. Others die slowly—alcohol, eating disorders, workaholism, and silence."

I survived, but not without cost. I know the price intimately:

- Sitting in the school bathroom, doubled over from pain 'down under,' a term I later upgraded to recurrent urinary tract infections (UTIs.) Still frequent, still awful—but at least there are now AZO test kits for self-diagnosis and treatment.
- Migraines so bad they made my head hit the desk in Spanish class. Great for a college app essay, not great for the GPA.
- Restless Leg Syndrome, known lovingly as RLS. It is so severe that I could have kept time for the percussion section—with my legs.
- Raynaud's Syndrome that turns my fingers dark blue whenever a boss or bureaucrat corners me with unjust demands, like giving an 'A' to a student who hadn't earned it.

The gift that keeps on giving. Thanks to my counselor—and truthfully, to finally learning about PACE—I started to understand.

I wasn't broken.
I was built under pressure—literally.
Molded by survival, definitely not safety.
The plans My Father had before I was born?
Interrupted.
His blueprint?
Built on manure.

You patch the cracks with what you've got, not what got flushed. You find the sturdiest scraps, the ones that survived. You keep building—piece by almost-matching piece—even if some of the pieces weren't yours to begin with.

That's the hidden toll of childhood trauma. Not just the bruises or broken trust. It's what it costs you long after the abuser is gone; the invisible tax on health, the overtime of emotional labor, the exhaustion of constantly rebuilding what should've been sturdy in the first place.

I didn't have language for it—not really—until I sat in that glowing, crystal-lit office with the counselor I met by stuffing raffle tickets into a jar labeled Wisdom. She didn't just talk. She listened and shared an understanding of PACE.

It changed everything.

Chapter 6
No Surprises, Please

Surprises can be fun. Surprise—new car with a big ribbon. Surprise—your college student is home for the holidays—let's just hope he didn't drop out. Surprise—you won the Mega Millions lottery—but you didn't buy the ticket.

Some people love surprises. They pivot well. Not me, OK…maybe if I won the real lottery—the Mega One.

In my life, 'surprise' sounds more like:

There's a puppy—you didn't ask for—in the trunk of the car.

You're not going back to university—because you weren't a 'good girl.'

Your son has a tumor the size of a softball in his skull.

Wake up—it's time to be abused.

Just once, I'd like:

Surprise! You're going to Disneyland.

Better yet, Surprise! You won a Grammy.

Surprises may catch everyone else off guard. For me, they trigger a full-body shutdown. Cortisol floods. My hands turn navy blue. My mouth breaks out in ulcers. My head starts to pound. My body keeps score—and then adds interest.

I never knew when I'd have to duck from a slap that came from nowhere. I never knew when the pain between my legs would make me sob in the girls' bathroom. I never knew when My Father would throw me across the room—right in front of the general's son—for sitting outside at 9:01 p.m. Yes, the very, very cute general's son. I never knew if My Father would pull me from a full room of people just to fondle me. I never knew when my bedroom door would creak open in the dark. Or if a pillow would be shoved over my face because I cried for help too loudly.

No—I didn't grow up with surprise parties. I grew up with surprise violence. And now, as a grown-up, I live with surprise betrayals.

After years of trauma, betrayal, and silent damage, I finally had protection through a 504 Plan at work—a legal document that outlines accommodations under the Americans with Disabilities Act. Not as a child in school but as an employee in the workplace.

You'd think all educational institutions that execute and oversee thousands of these accommodations would know how to follow them.

They don't.
Or maybe they just won't.

One of my simplest accommodations was:
No Surprises.

Let me know ahead of time. Don't make me wait for a response. Give me a chance to prepare. Show me you value me by giving me answers. Give my body the gift of not being blindsided.

One day, after almost twenty years of building an award-winning high school choral and musical theatre program, I was told to report to HR.

When I was first called into HR, I thought maybe—just maybe—they were finally going to honor my 504. Maybe this was about collaboration. Maybe they were going to do it right this time.

I asked—again and again—for more information in order to prepare for no surprises. They said it was nothing. "Just a quick check-in," they said. "We want to see how the musical went."

Meanwhile, I waited. A week. With sores in my mouth and hands turning blue. "No surprises," I reminded them. "It's no big deal," I told myself, "They just want a recap."

I arrived at the meeting prepared with my recap. Two central administrators and a vice principal were already seated. "The musical went great," I said, taking a seat. "You saw it. The reviews were awesome. You applauded. Everyone loved it."

The HR director didn't even blink, "You do know why you're here?" he asked, wearing a passive-aggressive smile. "To talk about the musical?" I responded. "NO, you're under investigation for harassment."

SURPRISE!
Big surprise!

Why couldn't it be, "Congratulations, you've won the Teacher of the Year Award! You're being recognized for your work with students and the music program." Nope.

I wasn't told what the specific complaints were—just that a complaint was filed and I was now under investigation. It was time to sit through a gauntlet of questions that I must defend myself against, all while being physically ready to throw up and my fingers turning blue.

After what seemed like an eternity, the interrogation came to a close. I was instructed not to tell anyone about the meeting or the investigation. Anything considered retribution toward the accuser would be regarded as terms for discipline. Retribution? What did that even mean? Does that mean being a 'good girl' and doing everything I was told?

Now, I was asked to be silent.
Again. What was happening?

I asked for a copy of the complaint. Eventually, an email with bullet points about cookies, programs, and my face was sent. Apparently, I had suggested that students not eat a giant chocolate chip cookie—gifted by the accuser—until after they sang. To be fair, chocolate causes mucus, making it harder to sing. Pure factual science. That's harassment?

I was told it would be resolved by the end of the month. Okay, but you do realize that waiting for the ax to fall is about 200 times harder for someone with complex PTSD? You do realize that's why I have a 504 accommodations plan on file, which acknowledges that waiting takes a physical and mental toll? And yet, I was reminded once more to tell no one.

To smile.
To teach.
To act like nothing had happened.

Four months later—with no communication, no closure, and my body breaking down from the stress—I received a letter in the snail mail—for you Gen X that is the United States Postal Service.

No harassment found. I had done nothing wrong. It was a 'personality conflict.' Meanwhile, I had been crying in the bathroom by day and throwing up by night. Too bad I don't lose weight from that.

One of the central administrators called me after I entered the 'afterlife.' She asked why I had retired sooner than planned—to be fair, I was old enough to draw Social Security.

But why did I truly decide to retire earlier than planned? Being accused of something so grievous, sitting around, and waiting for a conclusion had taken its toll. I didn't retire because of students, music, or the workload. Worse yet, if my 504 had been followed, all of the physical and psychological aftermath would never have happened.

Even now, as I write this, I can feel the cortisol rushing back. Butterflies under my skin. A migraine blooming.

>My body remembers.
>My body always remembers.

It would be easier not to tell this story. Easier to leave it buried with all the others. Here's the truth: Accommodations are not optional. They are not 'nice to have.' They are not about receiving special treatment. They are survival tools for people trying to function in a world that has already done real damage. 504 plans matter.

>For students.
>For employees.
>For survivors.

Shame on our abusers, but shame, too, on the people and systems that perpetuate the trauma long after the first blow has landed.

>So no.
>I don't love surprises.
>I love safety.
>I love knowing the plan.
>I love building a world in pieces I can see.

But sometimes…even the special pieces come in unmarked mystery bags.

Chapter 7
Unpacked

In my world, mystery bags don't mean surprise. They mean black duffels on a train. Or backpacks stuffed with camping gear—dragged home from the Appalachian hiking trails.

Camping and backpacking? Family favorites—subtract women, add dog.

Me?
Not so much.
Not my thing.
I usually say it's the heat. Or the bugs.

And while those are solid excuses, they're not exactly the truth. Believe it or not, it's not really the bugs. I once played tennis at night in Texas, squashing thousands of big, black, crunchy cicadas underfoot. Couldn't even see the lines. Didn't flinch.

It's not sleeping on the ground, either. Any sleep is good sleep when you've gone without it for years. I can thank school starting too early, my children, my Husband, my brother, and, of course, childhood.

And it's not even the 'camper potty.' Okay…that one. I do have issues with port-a-potties. Don't we all? Especially those of us who have to sit down.

The truth of why I might not like camping so much? It's being stuck in the middle of nowhere with no real way out. Doing all the cooking, cleaning, and grunt work—while fielding the nonstop stream of comments, requests, and instructions from everyone else.

Not that I haven't been camping.

Every summer, my mother packed me off to Girl Scout camp—an hour's drive from home. Sounds close, but in *Hawai'i*, that's far.

One year, I'd been really sick.

Most years, honestly—remember ACE? Adverse Childhood Effects.

This time was different.

Fever-of-104-degrees different.

Probably a gift from my weakened immune system—another little souvenir from My Father's abuse.

Regardless, my mother was bound and determined to send me to camp.

I remember begging—not metaphorically—my knees, hands together in prayer, begging not to go. I didn't feel well and was throwing up—a lot—worse than the night before I started the fifth grade in a new school. The story will be told in my next book—maybe.

Like I was saying, my mother insisted. She threw everything in the car and off we drove to Girl Scout camp. I was late, of course—by several days—because I'd had a fever. But it had been broken for at least an hour, so apparently I was good to go. I got there and was assigned a tent with three other girls. They had already bonded, so I was immediately the odd man out. Or the little girl with secrets at home who doesn't want to be at camp, sick and sad.

Within three hours, I was crying—big deal for me. I rarely cry—though more as I get older. I also had a fever. Again.

I dutifully reported to the nurse.

They called my mother.

Boy, was she mad.

She'd have to drive two hours—and miss out on her precious alone time. All of us who are moms can acknowledge needing our alone time. However, this was *my* mother.

The camp nurse insisted—just as my mother had done with me—that she come pick me up. Take me home.

I can imagine my mother muttering under her breath that I wasn't 'being a good girl.' Yet, even as a child, I remember thinking, "If I wasn't really sick, why would I want to go home?"

To *Him?*

Another year, I was sent to camp again. My memory of that year centers on a hike where campers were supposed to climb to the top of a mountain called Saddle Hill and spend the night—it was definitely not a hill.

I was not really sick—just the usual childhood trauma sick feeling—on that trip. I had washed my canteen cup—without adult supervision—and failed to rinse it properly. After hiking five miles in the *Hawai'i* sun, at a high elevation—carrying all my sleeping and eating gear, including a soapy cup—I rejoined the group. I might have been thirsty—or now we'd call it dehydrated.

I poured water into my 'clean cup.'
Soap bubbles appeared.
I took a sip.
It tasted like the soap my Grandma used to wash my mouth out with. It definitely didn't quench the dehydration.

I remember telling a grown-up.
And another.
No help.
No more water.

Full-on dehydration.
I ask myself, why don't I want to push my body and go backpacking?
Is it the bugs?
The outdoor latrine?
I could be that woman who was tough enough to tackle the outdoor elements.

That's worth something, right?

Maybe someday it will be worth trying.

Or not.

Recently, my Husband described a backpacking trip he took to the New Hampshire mountains. He explained the reason backpacking was so 'fun.'

Okay, I'm ready.

Seriously?

My fun and adventure are shopping with an unlimited budget, on someone else's credit card, and a Cosmo martini in my hand.

Yet, it seems to my Husband that fun is defined as pushing his body to the ultimate limit.

To his credit, he described a moment near the end of the trip—last two miles—when he didn't know how he could physically keep going. He believed there was nowhere safe to stop and camp—he kept going. When he finally reached the campsite, he collapsed, just like he does during his afternoon nap. Full out, can't move your big toe, collapsed. His declaration, "THRILLING."

Okay.

This is thrilling?

Try birthing four big babies—8.5, 7.95, 8, and almost 9-pounders—with no drugs. Did I mention the first time around was back labor, and during the last baby I bled out?

Hey, I got there.

Right?

I'm not afraid of bugs, hard work, or sleeping in the heat with mosquitoes and a soapy dish.

Actually, I am not afraid of much after My Father.

I explain it like this, "I don't need the thrill of 'let's see how close to death I can get.'" I faced that regularly as a child—and again during childbirth which, I'll admit, had much better results.

No, I don't camp.

I've already earned my merit badge in survival—without the tent. And if I'm going to haul gear through the wilderness, it better be metaphorical—and come with indoor plumbing.

I took the bruises meant for my siblings, protecting them from beatings. I used to sit for hours in the girls' bathroom at school, in pain from UTIs that were never treated. When I fought, I was smothered with a pillow until I lost consciousness. I was thrown across a room, and had migraines for days on end, while still expected to do life.

I will repeat one last time.
I don't need to push my body.

My Father already did that for me.

Measure 2
Animals, Chaos, and Coping

Chapter 8
Honey—The Dog
I Didn't Expect

As a child, my parents always had pets. My mother barely noticed them, at least no more than she did her own children. My Father pretended to care, but the pets always ended up outside on the lanai, ignored but fed.

Kelly was the first pet I really remember, though I've been told there was a little black poodle when I was born. I wonder what happened to her.

When we lived in California, Kelly slept near the bunkbeds my sister and I shared. She was a black, brown, and white collie—just like Lassie. Every noon on the dot, after kindergarten, she met me at the door like clockwork.

My school was right across the street from our little ranch house. I walked there every morning—alone—at five years old.

Then again…maybe I wasn't really alone.
Kelly was watching.

One day, my mother didn't make it home in time—from her bridge game, or shopping, or whatever she was doing—but Kelly was there. She sat at the edge of the road, watching for me to cross the street as if it were her job.

Is this Peter Pan of Neverland?

No, just a five-year-old girl and her shadow, covered in fur, waiting by the road.

When we moved to Hawai'i, I thought Kelly would come too. She could have. There was a quarantine system in place—she would have had to stay for a while. But My Father chose to send her 'somewhere' instead.

No goodbye.
No explanation.
Just gone.

Then came a stray named Pepper—black and white spots, found in a gully—the woods, for mainlanders. Her teats hung low from nursing. We went back to the gully and found five roly-poly puppies and carried them home, too.

Now that I think about it, Pepper might've belonged to someone.

Did my parents try to find out if she was someone else's? Not a chance. They just claimed her—like lost furniture left on the curb. Come to think of it, they once dragged an entire wooden playhouse out of that same gully for us to play in.

It, too, might've belonged to someone.

But possession was ten-tenths of the law in My Father's house.

And Pancake—the name I gave my favorite puppy—was now our possession, too.

She became my best friend. Every day after school, she greeted me with pure joy and elation.

We were inseparable. Soon, one by one, Pepper and her puppies vanished...until Pancake, too, was gone.

I had a seventh-grade project, and her name was Guin Elizabeth Pig—Guinea Pig, get it—Lizzy, for short. She was a long curly haired guinea pig. I loved her more than any dog.

She was fat, content, and always happy to snuggle.

I got an A on the project.

But My Father used to complain, "You love that guinea pig more than me. You even snuggle it when it's covered with poop. You won't snuggle with me."

First, let's be clear. My pets were never covered with poop, even when I was a child. And yes, I wanted to snuggle with Lizzy. And be an ocean away from My Father.

One day, I came home to an empty cage.
"Where's Lizzy?" I asked.
"Oh, she died," My Father replied.

Just like that.
Died.
"Died? Of what?"
"Her teeth were too big and she couldn't drink."
Really?

I felt devastated—but I couldn't show it.

Lizzyyyyyy!

You think that kind of loss can't repeat itself, that your heart might toughen up or shut down. But grief, like cruelty, always finds a way to evolve.

Tony (the Tiger) was my brother's Siamese cat with deep blue eyes and a knack for bedtime hide-and-seek. My Father would chase Tony down each night to hand him back to my brother.

One day, he 'disappeared' under the wheels of My Father's car.

Not long after Pancake came Honey.

My junior year of high school, My Father hollered, "Go get the groceries from the car!" When I opened the trunk, there she was. A half-Cocker spaniel, half-German shepherd puppy.

"Happy birthday," My Father said.

Except:

It wasn't my birthday. I hadn't asked for a puppy. I didn't even get to pick her out, though she was adorable.

He made it very clear she was mine to care for.

With Honey, I was handed a project and told, "Here—take care of her." A newspaper on the floor would magically house-train her. Or so I thought. Guidance or a book might've helped, but I hated reading—unless it was Holocaust histories that, for some reason, I devoured.

I named the new gift Honey for her golden coat. She had the lanky body of a shepherd and the soft face of a spaniel. She was mine. I slept with her and doted on her when I was home. I just wasn't home much.

At sixteen, I had one goal.

Leave.

Far away. Preferably by any means necessary, though college seemed the most acceptable choice at the time. Not the best plan to drag a forty-pound dog into a freshman dorm three thousand miles away.

A year later, I left Honey behind, promising I'd come back for her. She was banished the minute I flew away. Banished to where? The lanai, of course. Lonely, as always, even in a house full of people.

By then, the daughter My Father had abandoned—and her infant daughter—had both come to Hawai'i and moved in.

I can't make this up.

When I came home for breaks—no longer than two weeks at a time—Honey would hop into my lap, curl into a tight ball, and cry softly, gently gnawing on my hand.

She remembered me.

Until one day, she didn't.

I grieved for her, like she probably grieved for me.
I was older by then.

"She ran away," My Father announced. I understood better. He got rid of pets when the bond grew too strong.

Where was Honey?

A long time later, my mother's best friend spotted Honey rummaging through trash cans at an abandoned military base. When called, Honey ran straight to her.
A little digging revealed the truth.
My Father had dumped her and driven off.

I wish Honey could've lived out her days with the comfort I gave the pets I raised in my family.
When my children wanted a puppy, we did it the 'right' way—crate training, vet visits, dog books, the whole process. I think that's how it's supposed to work, right? Parents modeling, guiding, and helping their kids learn?

That included Kai's bearded dragon named Cling.
Kai left to couch-surf across the U.S. continent—a story for yet another book that he would never approve.

Nevertheless, Cling was left behind. No warning. No looking back. Every day I fed and checked on her.
A cold-blooded spiky lizard, dog-like in her devotion, whose highlight of the day was a handful of squirming super-worms. Not my best moment. Although feeding LIVE worms might've won me Mother of the Year.
One day, during a daily check, I noticed her skin hanging extremely loose. She wasn't even moving toward the squirmy worms. I immediately took her to the vet. The truth is, I couldn't let Kai's pet die on my watch.

I wrapped her tight in a towel and drove one-handed to the vet.

The $100 diagnosis?

"She's depressed. She needs more love."

A hundred dollars?

At least I found out Cling was a female. I suppose that is some consolation.

A lizard needs love?

Who knew?

So help me, for the dear lizard's life, I went home and placed that cold-blooded creature on my warm chest every night and loved her back to life.

She lived.

Because some things I know for sure.

Cling was a survivor.

Honey was a survivor.

And so am I.

Chapter 9
Rusty the DOG–I Didn't Want

When you think you're dying, everything looks different.

It started with a routine physical. You know, the kind you schedule so you can collect those extra bucks from 'the company.' My doctor called a week later with the results and explained, "Everything looks great—even better than last year."

Of course they did.

I'd been working hard in dance class and 'old-people'— alright, over 55–water aerobics class. I was kicking my way through five chronic neurological conditions gifted to me by childhood trauma—and the occasional piña colada.

Then came the "but."

Like the little room, you never want the "but"—not to be confused with butt, which I don't want either.
"There's a shadow on your chest X-ray," my primary care doctor informed me.
"We'd like you to get a CT scan."

Wait—what?
What about dance class?
What about "Better than last year"?
YOU LIED.
Very familiar territory.

I don't panic—I assess.
I act.
I survive.
I step up in a crisis.
I'm the fighter, remember?

I showed up for the CT as scheduled, dressed in my best "let's get undressed for a magnetic picture" outfit. No jeweled accessories, of course.

For five days, my body had been on full alert.

Then the lovely lady at the front desk told me the insurance company hadn't 'approved' the CT yet. I'd need to reschedule.

What do you mean by reschedule?

I am here now.

I drove thirty minutes in rush hour.

I mentally prepared to lie still and pretend I wasn't terrified—and you can't even take the picture?

Take a breath.
Remember, problem solve.
I immediately asked, "How much?"
Nothing money can't fix, right?
Or so I often think.

The tech looked at me like I was crazy—a frequent occurrence in my life. We have already established I am a little *pupule*. I assured the woman, who smiled a little too much, that if the insurance company wouldn't pay, I would. I wasn't thinking about money. I had a health savings account (HSA) padded with years of unused sick days—fifty bucks a day, stacked up from the 'before life.' You know, back when I showed up no matter what. Vomiting included.

She handed me the forms.
I signed my life away.
And off to the talking machine I went.

All that hullabaloo for three minutes of listening to a deep male voice calmly telling me,
"B…R…E…A...T…H…E."

Like, I don't already know how?
Or practice daily?
I am a choir director and survivor.

I'll admit it. I enjoyed the deep, calming, male voice. Little did I know, I'd practically be dating that voice for the next year.

Unlike during most of my sixty-something years, there are now medical portals. These new websites are fully stocked with panic. You can view all medical records that have your name on them.

Another one of those 'you like it' or 'you hate it' scenarios.

Now I could see the picture.
So I looked.
A swear word comes to mind at this point.

Nodules.
And something the doctor called "ground glass."

Then came the radiologist's note,
"Possible malignancy."

For those who don't speak radiology, that's code for CANCER. A phrase that implies you shouldn't panic while you're totally panicking.

The next thing you know, I found my Husband crying.

Yes, real tears.

Wet and sticky.

The first time I'd seen that kind of emotion in over forty years.

How sweet.

How touching.

How…'foreign'—like a melody drifting in from somewhere you didn't know existed.

He truly loves me.

And, for a moment, it reminded me of the only other time I'd seen him cry. That was many years ago in college, sitting on my couch, after five different guys had shown up at my door—at the same time.

I thought then he had cried because he realized he might love me. Because he might lose me. Turns out, he cried because he didn't feel special.

This time I asked, "Are you crying for me? Or for yourself?" I held my breath, hoping for an answer that would make me feel loved, valued. He paused. "I don't know," he replied, shaking his head and turning back to his office.

Time to continue the original story.

Maybe I was dying—but all I could think was;

"If this is it, I need to take my granddaughter to meet her Aunties in Hawai'i"—check.

"I need to bring Kai home for a visit from living abroad"—check.

"I need to build those shelves in the family room finally"—check.

"I need to build that swimming pool in my backyard"— I still need to check this off my to do list.

Even as I was trying to prepare for a possible conclusion to this life's journey, my heartstrings pulled hard toward the man I had married and loved for over forty years. The man I had attempted to lead a normal life with, despite having no role models to build upon. I couldn't leave him like this. I needed him to feel like he mattered.

What do you think I did next?

No, he didn't get a second wife or that motorcycle he pretended to desire after reading *Zen and the Art of Motorcycle Maintenance*.

After years of begging—and begging, and begging—I gave in to a PUPPY.

A very expensive puppy.

Nothing says, 'I love you,' more than a puppy.

The dog he'd always wanted.

I need to establish—and you to understand—I had already taken care of thousands of students AND their parents, four kids in a house full of chaos, a bearded dragon, several cats including; Boots, Roland, Poopsie, PITA— that stood for pain in the ass—AND a Bichon Frisée dog named Miss Muffin who lived seventeen years. By the way, my Husband names the animals and I named the children.

I didn't want anything else to be responsible for. Not when I was finally trying—really trying—to take care of myself. In these afterlife years, I was done with caretaking.

But it happened. I spent too much money on the puppy and all the paraphernalia recommended by the pet broker. Drove to the middle of Amish country in a snow shower to pick up an eight-pound, twelve-week-old, long-haired tweeny dachshund—with eyes too big for his tiny face and paws that didn't quite know what to do yet.

Yes, a wiener dog. A long, funny animal that barely looks like a dog. That's what my Husband had wanted all these years.

He named him Rusty.

Rusty turned out to be the best gift I ever gave him. He fell head over heels for Rusty.

That little dog is carried everywhere. Photographed like a celebrity. Fed like royalty. Spoken to like a soulmate.

AND THEN, a few weeks later, I found out I was NOT dying. Well, we're all dying—but not the 'buy him a dog' type of dying.

The sixty tumors weren't fast-growing cancers.

Just miserable little spots destined to make me feel like garbage while I waited month to month to find out if it was slow cancer, a fungus, or just lungs wrecked by years of surviving.

Which meant I was now stuck with the dog.
I was not thrilled.

My Husband swore up and down that I'd fall in love with the dog—which, for the record, I was still calling "DOG." He insisted Rusty would "choose" me. That I'd turn into one of those women obsessed with their little dog, dressing it in sweaters and taking selfies like we were BFFs—aka best female friends—oh…Rusty is a male, oops.

Not even close.

I was still exhausted—physically and emotionally—in that "don't start wrecking my house again" kind of way. I'd just started to recover from decades of kids, pets, and general destruction. I wasn't about to let a dachshund restart the cycle.

Then things slowly shifted. Not dramatically—but like when one brick clicks into place and suddenly the whole structure holds.

My Husband brought Rusty into his mother's new care facility room. She looked up at me, clear-eyed for the first time in days, and said, "I haven't seen my son this way since he met you. And now he has his Rusty. Thank you."

And in that moment, I softened. A little. Not because I suddenly wanted to be a dog mom. But because I saw something in that room: someone I loved, loving something so purely that it healed a part of him I never could.

Rusty stayed.

I didn't want another piece in the chaos, but it turns out that "DOG" snapped into a space I didn't even know was open.

And yes—every time my sister-in-law sees us now, she sings like she is performing in a Broadway chorus:
"Sheri loves the doggy..."
"SHERI loooves the dogggy..."
"SHERI LOOOOVES THE DOGGGGY..."

She's not wrong.
I just won't admit it out loud.

Chapter 10
Bad Behavior

Like most people who've lived through real trauma, I have several triggers.

The biggest one?

Bad behavior.

Though not in the sense most folks imagine—children's temper tantrums, teenagers being snarky, kids acting out.

I'm referring to adult bad behavior.

The everyday kind.

The kind that gets overlooked or excused.

The kind that slowly chips away at your soul.

It bothers me—no, triggers me—when people lie, manipulate, or exclude others. When they gossip, freeze others out, or smile while inflicting damage. When they hide cruelty behind manners, use passive-aggressive tactics, or weaponize silence.

It's the kind of behavior that doesn't make headlines. But it destroys people just the same. And truthfully? It's even more devastating when you're hypervigilant.

Because I don't miss the slight.

I hear the change in tone.

The whisper behind the door.

I see the rolling of eyes.

I know when I've been ghosted by an alumnus after lending him $200 when he was in a bind.

When people play games.
It's not just cruel.
It's insulting.
You think I don't notice? Please.
I notice everything—almost.

I saw it at school with students who'd survived the loss of friends and staff to suicide. Administrators always responded the same way, "They need trained staff," they'd say.

Translation: Counselors—who spend their days in offices making schedules and barely interacting with students—were the only ones deemed qualified to talk about suicide.

Even when traumatized students are crying in your room—vulnerable children who don't trust anyone else.

It's still, "Say nothing. Do nothing."

It wasn't a conversation.
It was a directive.
Repeated.
Unquestioned.
Don't get me started.

I watch bad behavior everywhere. The way people at the exercise club—who think they're better—whisper about others. Those who offend people for being a different race or sexual identity. People forcing their children into med school. Don't get me wrong, if your kid dreams of being a doctor, more power to them.

One weekend, I was dancing my heart out to Madonna and Bruno Mars in dance class. Then a self-important participant told the instructor during a water break—three feet away from me, like I wouldn't hear, even without hypervigilance—that she didn't like my dancing.

She complained that I was "annoying."

That he should control it.

"Especially all the fluffy stuff."

Fluffy stuff?

Do you mean the ballet pirouette?

The hula hip sway?

At least I can follow the beat—and the instructor.

Just saying.

As expected, my 'Guardian Angel' instructor only gave a small nod, pretending it was nothing. Yet I could see him simmering—shimmying and spinning—with even more flair than usual. I might have even seen steam coming out of his nose, which is saying something for a guy with such a positive aura.

When her gossip and snide comments didn't land, she doubled down. She wore a designer jacket— embroidered, of course, and no, it isn't cold inside, nor are we in Monte Carlo— and a baseball cap, not the kind real athletes wear—it had rhinestones no less. She seemed to be auditioning for Real Housewives of Passive Aggression while everyone else was in yoga pants and t-shirts—albeit most were Lululemon.

Another twig-thin trophy wife decided it was her mission to put me in my place. We were now strutting across the floor— part of dance class tradition—and, let's be real, we weren't models cat walking down a runway. I moved more like an overweight anteater—with rhythm.

She deliberately followed me.

Bumped into me.

Repeatedly.

Luckily, our instructor—who I swear has hypervigilance too—unexpectedly changed direction, probably intentionally. Now 'bumping into me lady' looked like a lost giraffe.

Thank goodness others see it—the gossip, the glances, the passive-aggressive landmines that quietly blow up the confidence of anyone daring to take up space.

They understand how that kind of bad behavior doesn't just bruise egos—it wrecks what the instructor, or director, is trying so hard to build: confidence, connection, and community. A space where people move or sing not just in rhythm, but in safety.

And when someone tries to shatter that with a look or a whisper? It's not just rude—it's sabotage. My guardian angel—in that moment—didn't let it slide, as though reminding me it deserved to matter.

Some of the hardest moments in life don't come from strangers. They come from the people we love. The ones who mean well but miss the mark.

It was clear my mother-in-law didn't have much time left. Ours was never a warm relationship, and that is saying it kindly. Still, I wanted her to have what everyone deserves—dignity, comfort, and a little peace in the end. To do that, I needed to be around the in-laws—what I lovingly call "the other side."

We'd never quite clicked.

And, truth be told, even my side—my Husband, kids, the whole crew—sometimes find me…a lot. Not in a bad way. Just—layered.

Growing up with trauma doesn't exactly make you light and breezy. You adapt. You read the room. You react fast. You don't always come off as easygoing. I'm not everyone's cup of tea—more like espresso with a side of cayenne.

I walk into a room and the energy shifts—sometimes warmer, sometimes more like a thunderstorm. It's pretty much accepted; you either love me or hate me. There's not a lot of middle ground. Most people have already made up their minds. But what hit me hardest was this: Some of the people I thought knew me best never really heard me at all.

There we were—me, the in-laws, and my fading mother-in-law—crammed together in a 1,200-square-foot 'villa' in a retirement community. A very cozy stage for emotional fireworks—please, don't let me end up in a place with only old people.

One night, in the cozy surroundings, my brother-in-law became enraged when I disagreed with his views on whether people should still have children in this broken world. Okay, yes, it's broken. But that's no reason to stop having children. If anything, we need to protect them from bad behavior.

He thought the world had been cruel to him. He felt interrupted—by me. And he exploded. He has his own triggers. I know what that looks like.

However, trauma doesn't give you a free pass to kick over someone else's building project just because yours got destroyed.

The real damage doesn't come from outbursts. It comes in the quiet, calculated, aftermath. The whispered side conversations. The disinvitations. The sudden exclusion from meals and decisions.

It's not new. It's what happens when people want to hurt you without confrontation. When they make you feel small and unworthy. When they feel insecure, they try to manage it by making you feel smaller. That's adult bad behavior: strategic cruelty in polite dress.

Pretend nothing happened?
Say nothing?

Not me.

I've spent too many years swallowing silence to keep the peace.

Peace built on silence isn't peace at all—it's a control and power game.

I am trying not to do that anymore.

I'm trying to name things for what they are.

To speak up.

To walk out.

To stand taller, even when the ground beneath me shakes.

Because bad behavior doesn't get better when you excuse it, it only gets bolder.

And I've earned the right to be here—on my own terms.

Chapter 11
I Watched

I realize I have been blessed in so many ways when I open my eyes and simply watch. Even when my real eyes aren't cooperating. Those specialized hard lenses never quite fit my stubborn corneas—but at least they're a pretty shade of blue. Anyway, back to what I actually see.

I've watched the rain and the ocean wash the ugly away.
I've watched strangers become closer than family.
I've watched laughter return where silence used to live.
I've watched my students and choir members find their voices and my daughter find her strength.

And lately, I've been watching time itself—how it folds old moments into new ones, how it moves forward whether I'm ready or not. Especially now, as I prepare to launch a book that I know won't make everyone happy. Maybe that's what becoming a Glamma—what my grandchildren call me—means: learning to watch with both gratitude and ache, to see beauty even when it hurts.

As a child, I watched the rain in *Hawai'i* wash the ugly away, though sometimes it felt like it might wash everything away—including me. Between my years in public school, I spent the middle years—fifth through eighth grade—at a private one, HBA (Hawai'i Baptist Academy). Several of my HBA teachers had studied at Baylor and were the first to tell me about it.

Both the elementary and new Pali secondary buildings had been built on streams. When winter came, the tears of heaven—the rain—would fill the gullies and streams until they overflowed, rushing downhill toward the ocean.

My classmates were often frightened, but I somehow felt peace and was drawn to the rushing water. Maybe because it reminded me of my own soul—fast-moving, secret, and finally free. I didn't have a name for it then. I just knew that watching was safer than speaking. I was studying beauty and chaos at the same time.

In fifth grade, I joined the Junior Police Drill Team. We practiced every Wednesday after school. Even so, we were the worst team on the island. Once, we went on a field trip to *Ala Moana* Beach Park, right across from the shopping center—still my favorite place to swim when I stay in town. I love watching the local families of many generations set up their tents and grills, filling the park with food, laughter, and music.

We were there for the state championship, though I'm still not sure why we were invited—probably because it is a small state. I watched the precision of teams from public schools and wished our small uncoordinated group of misfits could do the same thing. I was secretly hoping the noise at home would quiet and be replaced by the order and certainty of a drill team.

On Wednesday nights, I needed to get home, but my parents didn't want to make the long drive to town to pick me up. It turned out to be a blessing. A local single mother—I thought ancient at the time—and her daughter lived behind the school in a cramped, messy, apartment. I was to go and stay with them after practice, and they would drive me to church to meet my mother. This was before my mother knew she could have me ride 'da bus' for two hours and transfer on Hotel Street—Honolulu's red light district.

As I entered the home I saw piled magazines and laundry on the couch, and a TV blaring with the local news. Yet, somehow, I felt love and peace. Unlike my own house, which looked neat and tidy but hid chaos, this one looked chaotic but welcomed me with open arms and quiet order.

Each week, a home-cooked meal was shared with me. I stood near the woman, shoulder to shoulder in the small kitchen, while she prepared traditional island meals. It was where I learned to use chopsticks and to eat sticky rice with tempura or fried noodles and vegetables. She would make battered fish, and the small apartment would fill with the smell of oil and warmth. Even now, that memory brings comfort to my heart. That kitchen, that woman, that small act of care—it was the first place I watched chaos really be full of peace.

As a young adult I was pregnant in a rural town in the Ozarks—a place that barely showed up on a map but somehow held my entire world. My Husband was finishing graduate school at the state university while I taught third grade thirty miles away in what most people would call nowhere. But it was somewhere.

The administrator of the one-school district hired me even though he knew I was pregnant and might only stay a year or two before moving. That act alone told me who he was. He never yelled or belittled anyone. He led with calm, quiet integrity—the kind that didn't need to prove itself.

It seems contrary, but in those days society said it was acceptable to use a paddle. I never thought it was alright, but he was still a good man and a fair administrator—shaped by the norms of his time. Once, when I brought a student to his office for misbehavior, he calmly reached for the paddle that hung on the wall. I was horrified. Poor Billie Joe didn't need punishment; he needed love. I never sent another child to his office.

I would learn later that Billie Joe came from an abusive home—a dirt-floor shack near a stream that sometimes flooded so badly he couldn't cross it to get to the bus stop. Looking back, I realize he wasn't difficult; he was surviving. Years later, when I began to understand the lasting impact of childhood trauma, I thought of him often. How easily we label a child 'defiant' when what we're really seeing is fear.

How many Billie Joes I must have taught before I learned to look deeper.

There wasn't much mentoring back then. We figured things out as we went, borrowing worksheets from each other and running them through the mimeograph machine that left our fingers stained blue. That same little room—crowded with paper, fumes, and noise—was where I'd pump breast milk from a fifteen-dollar hand pump I bought at Walmart. I never felt embarrassed; it was just what working mothers did to make it all fit.

Because the $9,000 a year I earned didn't stretch far, I drove every day with three other teachers who also lived about thirty miles away. The school was a rectangular building that housed one classroom per grade with an attached gym on one end and a cafeteria on the other. No frills. We took turns behind the wheel, talking and laughing the whole way. We shared stories, lesson plans, and sack lunches—and that year, all four of us were pregnant. Every morning, we compared swollen ankles, exhaustion levels, and baby names. Those rides became our little moving sanctuary, a place where we could be teachers, mothers, and friends all at once.

My neighbors were kind too—even when I ran across the yard one afternoon screaming that their cow was dead because it was lying on its side and not moving. At that same moment, the cow stood up, looked at me, and walked away. My neighbor just laughed, handed me a jug of milk from that same cow, and told me I was doing fine. I needed it. I was living on thirty-three-cent macaroni and cheese made with only water. Forty years later I would knock on the same door and the neighbor answered like I had insisted the cow was dead yesterday.

Then there was my family practice doctor, who reminded me at a Christmas party a week before my daughter's birth that I had requested no medication during labor. I'd actually told him that in my written birthing plan. It was the year I believed a book could teach me everything and that I would be the kind of mother who did it all naturally—no matter what. I had no idea.

During back labor, I grabbed him by the stethoscope, pulled his head down, and yelled, "I WANT DRUGS!" He just smiled and patted my knee. "We discussed this at the party," he said, and walked away.

Hours later, when my eight-pound, fifteen-ounce daughter finally arrived, everything went still. The pain, the chaos, the indignity of that so-called 'natural' birth—all of it faded the moment I held her. I promised nothing would ever hurt her. Of course, life had other plans. But I gave her every tool I could to become the strong woman she is today.

Now I'm reminded of the thousands of students I've taught and the countless memories that live somewhere between my heart and the book I had made by Artkive. It holds pictures, notes, and mementos gathered alongside the digital trail of iTunes, old mp3s, and YouTube clips that hold fragments of those years.

I still cherish the sound of voices rising together.

The smiles that grow a little bigger each week.

The laughter that fills the room, especially the moments when my dry humor finally earns real laughs instead of eye rolls.

I cherish story time, and the way my grandchildren's faces light up when I walk through the door—well, except for the middle schooler, who mostly offers a nod.

The joy of flying Delta One with my granddaughter and discovering *Hawai'i* together.

Birthday celebrations that always end with homemade cake and double the frosting.

I cherish quiet mornings looking out over the pond, and the kind of laughter with friends that isn't about forgetting pain, but about celebrating life—its silliness, its surprises, and the simple joy of being together.

Recently, at a Care House gala, I watched an incredibly strong eleven-year-old walk to the podium beside her grandmother and tell her story of survival—and the role CARE House played in helping her heal. I felt both heartbreak and awe. There she stood, brave and sure, doing what so many of us take a lifetime to do: speaking the truth out loud.

At Thanksgiving, I set the table with the ninety-dollar china I bought at an estate sale—I didn't get any for my wedding. And the silver I once hid from my *pupule* cousin—I did say it ran in the family—that had belonged to my aunt. He would have sold it, along with everything else she had lovingly cherished, to an estate dealer for four thousand dollars—just to have the cash and move off-grid. I have no idea where he is now, and I've stopped looking.

Every time I take it out and set the table, I think of her— one of the hundred WACs (Women's Army Corps) in military intelligence during World War II and one of the first women to graduate from Columbia Law School. Her career ended as one of the top lawyers for the Veteran's Administration. Quite an achievement. I try to honor her, and maybe keep her alive a little longer in my grandchildren's memories, by using her silver.

One Thanksgiving, my grandson looked at the table and asked why it looked so "royal." Everyone laughed, but I knew the answer. Each year, when I set that table, it isn't just dinner. It's a tribute to the strong women who came before me, and to the girl who finally learned how to watch for beauty instead of waiting for permission.

Sometimes I still see that fifth-grade girl, standing in the rain, watching everything rush downhill toward the ocean.

But now, I understand—nothing I've loved has ever really been lost.

It just changes form, waits for me to notice, and keeps moving forward.

Chapter 12
Dorothy from Kansas

The opening scene of *Forever Young* depicts an older woman in a cozy bookstore, reading aloud from one of her many published books to a small crowd of adoring fans. She's eloquent, poised, and well-dressed—everything I dream of being. Well, except I'd probably fumble over every word and have the tag sticking out of the back of my dress.

Why am I watching a movie about a 'mature' book author reading to her fans?

Why aren't I writing instead?

I won't be able to read from my book if I never write the words down in the first place.

Why haven't I told my story yet?

Strangely, in that moment, the story that rose to the surface wasn't even about me. It was about Dorothy from Kansas—my mother-in-law.

We've already established that I was never Dorothy's favorite person. Not even for that hot minute during our first meeting—you know, the brief grace period before you've had time to mess things up. No honeymoon there.

The truth is, I didn't know the secret code—the rules of the midwest. Still not sure I do. I didn't know how to be the quiet, obedient version of 'nice' she expected.

The 'other side'—who, to be fair, hadn't exactly mastered social skills themselves—decided early on that I wasn't "Christian enough" or "midwestern enough" for the family, even though my boyfriend-turned-husband had already sworn off Christianity by then.

Maybe it was the part-Jewish thing. Okay—not technically. I am not Jewish under Torah law, but 29% Ashkenazi DNA wasn't exactly what the other side considered good Baptist stock from Kansas.

Or maybe it was because I was overdressed in *muumuus* and flip-flops—*Hawai'ian* fashion.

Or carefree.

Or outspoken.

Or opinionated.

Or maybe—and let's be honest, this is probably why—it was because I lifted my skirt at their 25th wedding anniversary party to show a group of Southern Baptist men the birthmark on my leg. I truly can't even tell you why I did it. It was my first visit with the family. Not my finest moment.

Things had gotten so hostile with the 'other side' of the family that my Husband finally announced, after more than thirty years, that I shouldn't go with him to his family's home—not even on holidays. He explained that his family had treated me so badly he was protecting me by keeping me home.

Maybe He was.
Maybe not.
Whatever the reason,
I was never part of the fold.

When Dorothy began to decline—91 years young, her body tired, her liver failing—I stepped in. Me, the daughter-in-law who didn't belong to the flock.

Dorothy from Kansas wasn't abusive—not like the kind of pain I grew up with. She didn't terrorize or destroy. She didn't fracture your identity or make you question your worth.

A member of the 'other side' blurted out, "She's mean," concluding with, "I don't even know why I love her."

Really? That's your complaint? A reason not to love your mother?

Try growing up in a house where silence was a weapon, and touch was never safe. Then get back to me. PLEASE.

She was just plain grouchy sometimes. Not the 'smother me with a pillow' sort of grouchy. Just mean enough. In their book.

In mine too.

I still showed up.

Dorothy didn't go out with some big, dramatic flourish. She just got quiet—probably from the morphine or not being able to express how she felt or what she wanted. She was tired and in pain. She slipped away.

Hawai'i has taught me so many things, but most of all: *Aloha*. In *Hawai'ian* culture, *kūpuna*—grandparents, ancestors, or revered elders—are cared for with softness and presence, even if they didn't always offer you the same. They are highly respected figures who hold and transmit generational knowledge and cultural wisdom to younger generations.

Dorothy was my *'Ohana*—family. The grandmother to MY children. Part of my fold, whether she liked it or not. And when family needs you, you show up. Even if they don't want you to.

I've been beaten up for doing the right thing more times than I can count. It's kind of my specialty. This time was no different. I asked questions. I pushed for care. I made sure she had what she needed in her hospice room:

Her motorized lounge chair.

Her teapot collection.

The paintings she loved.

The pictures of her husbands and her dog.

All the while, her children stayed away—wrapped in their own emotions. It didn't win me any popularity contests. Not with the other side. Not with the retirement facility staff. But I wasn't looking for another casserole. Or a Facebook shoutout. I just needed to be able to look at myself and say:

You didn't walk away.

Not this time.

Not even from her.

Dorothy didn't drink alcohol. Not even one sip in ninety-one years. Maybe it was that 1917 anatomy book I found on her shelf; the one that declared, in no uncertain terms, that a single sip would ruin you. Midwest—Kansas—values.

Dorothy didn't take many medications either. I do. The kind that keeps trauma survivors upright. Functioning. Breathing. The kind that holds wreckage together—at least for a while. The kind that slowly eats at your liver yet lets you walk into a hospice room with calm in your voice and a dog at your side.

That's the kind of strength no one sees. The type of love that doesn't get Hallmark cards. I stood up for a woman who'd spent years keeping her distance—maybe that's exactly why it mattered more.

I didn't show up because she deserved it. I showed up because I deserved to be the kind of person who shows up. Even when it's messy. Even when I'm not wanted. Because someday—when it's my turn to slip away—I want to know I didn't flinch. I want my people to remember that I stayed.

There's another scene in *Forever Young* when someone asks, "If you could go back...would you?"

If I could go back in time?

No. Please—no.

Not to my childhood.

Not to my child surviving in the ICU.

Not to forty-some years of teaching.

Not to just surviving day to day.

But I also know this. If even one thing had been different, some beautiful parts of my life might never have happened:

My children.

My students.

My music.

The grandchildren who dance through my Wednesdays.

The broken people I've loved—and who've loved me back—in their own imperfect ways.

It's not about building something perfect. It's about working with what's real—what's cracked and mismatched and unfinished—and making it matter anyway.

That's what I did for Dorothy from Kansas.

That's what I keep doing—one piece at a time.

Chapter 13
Leo the Lion, Born Year of the Tiger

Dorothy was gone.

Her teapots boxed up.

The hospice bed stripped and filled by another.

I was still sitting with the ache—not of guilt, but of being misunderstood. I had fought for her and I was still sitting with the weight of that fight.

It's funny how we convince ourselves—or let the people around convince us—that we're the problem. That we're too much. Too loud. Too emotional. Too complicated. That if we just stay quiet or stay home, everything will be easier.

Because we're damaged.

Because we're too much.

Because we're not enough.

They hand us the blame so easily, and we carry it like it's ours to hold.

That's how it was when I was a child.

My mother blamed me for not being a 'good girl' and not being dedicated to God enough. How many families told themselves the same thing as they sent their daughters off to the convent?

And My Father.

He went the other direction.

According to him, he had saved me.

Because otherwise, what would I have been?
A tease?
A whore?
Just another girl to use and discard?

Maybe that's why I couldn't stay quiet.
Why I didn't disappear.
Why I kept showing up—bruised, but standing.

Silenced.

Not just as a child. In my adult life, too. I never found a rescuer. No safe arms to fall into and finally exhale.

Most humans let me down. Not with fists. With silence. With whispers. With secrets. With the slow erosion of what it means to be seen.

Really seen.
Or chosen.
Or safe.

The kind of betrayal that doesn't leave bruises.
Just doubt.
And distance.
With the ache of not being truly seen.

When you grow up learning to adjust—to make yourself small, to keep the peace at all costs—you start to believe the silence is your fault. For a long time, I believed it was. But that's what trauma does. It rewires you. It trains you to adapt, to endure, to survive—even when your spirit is starving.

And I did survive. I held it together. I did what I always did. I made it work. I built something stable with the pieces I had.

Until one day, I stopped.
Stopped accepting silence as love.
Stopped apologizing for needing more.
Stopped believing the lie that I was too much, too loud,
or too broken to be chosen.

That story wasn't mine to carry.

I am not the villain.
I am not the victim.
Not anymore.
I'm a SURVIVOR.
What are the odds?

A Leo, born in the Year of the Tiger.
I wasn't made to disappear.

I was made to roar.

Measure 3
Truth and Turning Points

Chapter 14
Good, Bad, and Ugly

GRANDMA... Good

She was a baffling woman. Born in 1898 on a sharecropper's farm in Rome, Georgia, one of thirteen children, daughter of a Baptist preacher. She had three dresses: one for school, one for church, and one for "pickin' cotton," as she would say. She only made it through sixth grade, but don't let that fool you. She was smart. Smarter than anyone I knew as a child.

Her name was Laura. Laura Ruth. But everyone called her Ruth. I called her Grandma.

She broke the family mold and fell for a handsome rogue who'd come back to town for a grave cleaning. One look, and she was hooked. She married Russell, her true love—and I got to hear about that true love until the day she died. She had a ginormous-sized photo of her 'Russell' hanging on the wall like a shrine.

Ruth and Russell traded cotton fields for the city streets of Baltimore. Strict and God-fearing—not Grandpa—she kept the family afloat during the Great Depression. Russell worked for the B&O Railroad and gambled more than he should've. Grandma took in boarders, cooked, and cleaned for others—and hid the money. Thanks to her, all their children graduated from prestigious colleges.

By 1933 her family back in Georgia could barely put food on the table. She brought them to Maryland on a train—housing, feeding, and carrying them all.

Everyone.

She was a survivor.

My mother was born in 1938. Grandma was forty—ancient for childbirth back then.

During labor, the doctors asked Grandpa an unthinkable question, "Who should we save, your wife or your child?" I don't know how he answered. They both survived.

Grandma liked to say she never used birth control—just "left it in the Lord's hands." Her older children were sixteen and eighteen when my mom arrived.

When my mother met My Father—a divorced man with two kids he'd already abandoned—they married within three months. I don't know all the details, but I do know this: My grandparents were not thrilled.

Eventually, My Father was stationed in *Hawai'i*. After Grandpa died, Grandma made the long trip from Maryland to visit. No FaceTime. No Southwest Airlines. No overnight shipping. Just a woman born in 1898, flying across the continental U.S. and the Pacific Ocean like it was no big deal. Imagine that.

GRANDMA... Bad

When Grandma visited, she stayed for a while—a long while—six to nine months at a time. She slept on the lanai, helped raise us, and yes…did the disciplining.

If I said something like "shut up"—which I swear wasn't even a bad word—she'd wash my mouth out with soap. I still gag if I accidentally taste Dove soap. There was a worse punishment if I misbehaved or was disrespectful. She'd snap a switch off the tree to "teach me a lesson." My mom would tell me, "Be glad it's not a belt." We agreed to disagree on that one.

My legs were black and blue for weeks.

But I never doubted her love.

Not once.

GRANDMA... Ugly

"Don't be ugly," Grandma would say, usually right before the soap or switch.

As an adult, I've been diagnosed with restless leg syndrome (RLS)—one of the many gifts from my childhood trauma. I take medication now and sleep through the night, but Grandma didn't have that luxury.

At night, she'd roam the house rubbing Vicks on her legs, the air thick with menthol. I used to think her legs kept her moving. But later I wondered, was she restless or worried?

In fifth grade, it was decided I'd go back to the mainland with Grandma for a six-week trip to visit the massive southern branches of the Parris and Smith clans. We'd sightsee, attend family reunions and, at night, I'd sleep safely next to her.

It was the first time I'd ever left home. I wasn't scared of Grandma. I was scared of My Father. I had learned to expect the creaking door at night.

When we arrived at my Grandma's childhood home in Georgia, we stayed with her younger brother, whose grown son had Down syndrome. His name was Junior, and I'd heard about him my whole life. Even at eleven, I was inspired that his parents had refused to institutionalize him. Instead, they helped him work in a factory making stuffed animals.

Junior had once sent one of those stuffed animals all the way to *Hawai'i*—a blue dog—that became my brother's prized possession, even after it lost a leg from too much love. Junior was kind. And he wanted hugs—lots of them.

I was terrified.

And somehow, Grandma knew why.

She kept saying, "You're safe now. I'll protect you."

She *knew.*

She didn't protect me at home.

She didn't say anything.

That...is UGLY.

MY HUSBAND… Good

I had a class in college—*Literature After Burns.* The Romantics: Shelley, Keats, Byron. It was taught by an old-school literature professor who believed in rigor, respect, and alphabetical order. The lectures were in the Browning Library, named for another Romantic poet and, when you walked in, the magnificent marble foyer practically screamed class and tradition.

When the Baylor a Cappella Choir sang there, the sound amplified perfectly—clear, full, resonant. The acoustics were almost sacred.

When the professor seated us in alphabetical order, it felt like a literary roll call.

Unfortunately for me, my last name landed near the beginning of the alphabet—which meant aisle seat, third row from the front. Horrifying. At least to me. I've always believed the best seat in the house is in the back. That's where you can see everything—and be seen by no one.

Unless it's dance class, where I'm front and center—shaking my trauma loose like I'm auditioning for *Dancing with the Stars.*

In the afternoons I laid in the baby pool at the University activity center—yes, the same one usually occupied by staff's toddlers—baking under the scorching Texas sun. My skin turned golden brown; my long, wavy hair flowed down my back. It's now been edited for age and efficiency.

A tall, handsome, underweight guy with blond hair—thinning even then—and piercing blue eyes, sat right behind me. He didn't mind alphabetical order—he had a front-row view of tan skin and flowing hair. Or so he admitted later.

One day, I turned around from my alphabetically assigned seat and blurted out, "You look like my boyfriend." No idea why I said that.

"A lot of people look like me," he replied.

"No," I said emphatically. "I said *you* look like *my* boyfriend. Not that other people look like *you.*"

Then I spun right back around like nothing happened.

Weeks later, I'd taken an incomplete in the class. I rushed home to deal with a family crisis.

Always a crisis with my childhood.

I came back at the start of the fall semester with no clue what I'd missed—and somehow still had to take the final for the *Literature After Burns* course. Nothing says *Romantic* like panic, disorientation, and unresolved childhood trauma.

That same guy—who looked like my former 'boyfriend'—strutted across the quad. I chased after him, desperate.

"Can I borrow your notes? I really, really, really need help with the final."

The tall, thin blond said, "Meet me at my house next to Schlotzsky's at 4:30."

Yes! I'm going to get notes.

He got an A. I can get an A.

Except...he wasn't there at 4:30. Or 5:00. Or 5:15.

I waited—annoyed but desperate.

Finally, at 5:20, he showed up, bedraggled and apologetic. Someone had stolen his bike. He had no car, no money, and had just lost his only transportation.

"Life sucks," he exclaimed.

And I don't know why—maybe it was the exhaustion, frustration, or perhaps it was the Texas heat—but I just started telling him everything.

Not the deepest details.

Not the door without a lock.

Not full control.

But enough.

Enough for him to know my life wasn't like his.

He didn't judge.

He didn't pity.

He had never met anyone like me in his safe little midwest Baptist life.

That night, he wrote in his journal: I'm going to marry this girl.

Nine months later, on a Monday morning, we were married in a garden yard. It was attached to an antebellum house between two white gazebos, surrounded by an intimate group of family and friends. Not lavish, but deliberate.

The leis—*maile* and *pīkake*—had been flown in. *Hawai'ian* orchids filled the bouquets and the snack table centerpiece. My dress had off-the-shoulder sleeves, a cinched waist, and a delicate lace train.

I'd picked it out with my soon-to-be mother-in-law.

My mother was furious.

It poured rain for four days before and four days after. But for the brief hours of the wedding ceremony, the sun came out. Not ideal for walking across a soggy lawn in heels—that sank into the wet ground—but still, the timing felt like a kind of grace.

Just before walking me down the wet grass, My Father pulled a pair of scissors from his pocket. With one hand, he held out the credit cards I'd been given for college—then calmly sliced them into tiny pieces and let them flutter to the ground like dead confetti. Then he offered his arm and walked me down that same soggy grass like nothing had happened.

We stood beneath the open sky and spoke our vows— two imperfect people making a promise we didn't fully understand but meant with everything we had. It wasn't a fairy tale. But it was real. It was forty plus years ago.

My husband is brilliant. He works extremely hard. Everyone likes him. He runs the neighborhood water system—he had to get certified by the state water officials—with grace and diplomacy, like the mayor of our multicultural cul-de-sac.

He's a great father and the best grandpa I know. Our first grandson looks just like him—blond hair, green eyes. They sit around coding Python like it's recess. Level-headed and calm, he's the perfect counterweight to my PTO (parent teacher organization) Tiger-Mom instincts.

Okay, maybe I hovered a little.

We all know why.

So yes. To the outside world he's the guy who 'puts up with' the crazy woman.

Except I'm not crazy.

I just survived some sh*t.

MY HUSBAND... Bad

My Husband craves adventure. That's not necessarily a bad thing. Somehow, he is always up for a surprise—already established, I don't like surprises.

Maybe that's why he married me.

Adventure guaranteed. One night, I overheard him talking to our college-age son. I was supposed to be asleep.

"She's damaged," he said.

Excuse me?

I'm a trauma survivor.

I have triggers and hypervigilance.

But 'damaged?'

I confronted him and my son.

They "didn't mean it like that."

Sure.

Sometimes—you never know…until you do.

MY HUSBAND… Ugly

All marriages have their Good, their Bad—and then there's the Ugly.

The Ugly is quieter—colder.
It's punishment—without yelling.
It's betrayal—disguised as independence.

There's no scoreboard—just silence, distance, and a quiet certainty that whatever went wrong was probably my fault.

He won't argue—he avoids conflict at all costs. He wants to be seen as the good guy. And maybe, to the outside world, he is.

It's not a disagreement. It's a slow unraveling—until you don't even trust your own voice.

It's not dramatic.
It's eroding.

That's Ugly.

MY FATHER… Good

My Father, Good?

I know. You're surprised.
Remember—I don't like surprises.

It's true. He did some good things. Life is often a contradiction—certainly mine. Of course, I'll admit, it all benefited *him* in some way.

He brought electricity to his third wife's Filipino fishing village—he threw in McDonald's cheeseburgers for the whole town, too—yummy.

He helped hundreds of businesses 'succeed' through his innovative bookkeeping—and a few of those businesses got a crash course in 'creative accounting' as well.

He taught me to play golf and tennis like a pro. And on Sundays, while the rest of the family was off singing praises to God, he made brunch.

My Father was the second child of three, all born within three years, right in the middle of the Great Depression. By the time he was four, his parents were divorced, and his father had disappeared for good.

Life wasn't easy. He was cold, hungry, and mistreated in foster homes. His mother eventually remarried, but that didn't improve things much.

Still, he dreamed big.

He wanted to be a Naval officer and go to the Naval Academy. He applied—with a Jewish last name he barely understood, inherited from the man who'd abandoned his mother—and he was rejected.

But he's not a quitter.

Believe me, I know that firsthand.

He enlisted. Legally changed his name to that of his stepfather. Applied again. This time, he got in. Four years later, he graduated and got married in the chapel at Annapolis.

He's been married three times.

Wife #1—I don't even know her name.

Wife #2—My mother. I'll leave it at that.

Wife #3—A woman eleven years younger than me, selected from an old-school, hardcover mail-order bride catalog. They've been married 25 years now. She gets all the Gucci bags, the Porsche merch, and the house he 'sold' to her—so he could claim he was broke. I call her Gucci Girl.

In 2014, after decades of silence, he called with a stock tip:

"Buy Tesla." I didn't. Probably the one time I should've listened.

Did I mention he has no money? LOL.

Anyway—off topic.

The point is:
Yes. He did some good.

MY FATHER... Bad

My mother had a long-held secret. "You have a half-brother and sister," and added, "Your Father was married before me." He had abandoned his first two children. My half-sister didn't see him again until she found him on her own at 21.

My half-brother? I met him once. I don't even know if he's still alive. Heard he was killed in the drug wars in the '90s—I can't make this up.

Truth be told…
I doubt my father knows where he is either.

My Father lies about money. He has called the police multiple times on his homeless son—the same one who grew up in that house—just for coming in to steal a Navy Marine golf hat before My Father dies. So wrong on all levels.

My Father threatens me whenever I try to reconnect with old friends from 'His block'—what my students used to call my "hood" after we did a drive-by tour of my childhood neighborhood.

This isn't just bad parenting.
It's bad character.

MY FATHER... Ugly

The worst?
He abused me.

Mentally.
Physically.
Sexually.

He didn't want a daughter.
He wanted a possession.

Something he could shape, own, erase.
And for a while, he did.

NOT forever.

I didn't just survive him.
I outgrew him.
Outlived the version of myself he tried to make.

I was never his ugly duckling.
I was never his at all.

I am mine.
A lion.
Born Leo, Year of the Tiger.
And I bite back.

That's the Good. The Bad. And the Ugly.

All of it shaped me. None of it defined me.

I don't live in the past.
But I don't rewrite it either.

This life? I built it.
Without blueprints.
Without permission.
With what I had.

Chapter 15
Mr. Greene

I didn't see it coming.

Micah Greene was brilliant. Smart, sharp as hell, and weird in the best way. Complicated.

He was the drama teacher and TV production director at the high school where we both gave our money, our time, our energy—simply, our hearts.

We were creative partners, co-conspirators, and, eventually, friends. I might've called him my work husband if I weren't twenty years his senior.

Like any long marriage, we laughed, cried, argued, yelled, and wrangled kids together.

Not everyone got him. His style wasn't polished or predictable. He was intense. Sarcastic. Sometimes off-putting. Underneath all that, he was electric. He made things matter. He cared. About the work. About the kids. About doing something real.

Vocal auditions for the spring musical were the last week of February. It was his return to directing after some time away, and we—at least I—were excited to dive back in.

We'd produced big shows together before: *Beauty and the Beast, Children of Eden, Les Misérables*, even *Ragtime*, complete with a real Model T on stage and a loud realistic prop gun.

Pippin was perfect for us: theatrical, weird, full of metaphor—which he had picked on purpose—and rich with music and possibility.

Micah had paid extra so our student pit, which I directed, could get the scores early to learn. These amazing students had already learned the entire show. It was time for the singers to audition. Everything was ready to go.

And then…he didn't show up.

That morning, Micah called everyone.
The office. The secretary. Other teachers.
He made excuses. Covered his tracks.

Not for me.
He didn't call me.

That's how I knew.

He had decided it was time. That day. That exact day— the one I had looked forward to. The one that was supposed to be the beginning of something new, something creative, something chaotic, something joyful.

When he didn't show up, I called HR to find him. I set up a camera to record the auditions. The show must go on. At least that's what I told myself. Because when things fall apart, I build. I organize. I steady the ship. Even if I'm the one taking on water.

The phone call came just minutes after the auditions ended. His hand-picked replacement—an alumna, not much older than the kids—was already waiting in the wings. She didn't know. Not really.

But somewhere deep down, I think I did.
Not the details. Not the plan.
Just the feeling.
The absence.
The silence.
The space he usually filled.

That day, while I was still at school,
Micah chose to end his life.
And he didn't say goodbye.

I don't know if it was intentional.
But it felt intentional.
It feels intentional.
It feels personal.

That's what grief does. It lies to you. It tells you the pain
was aimed at you. That the silence was a message. The absence
was a punishment.

That evening, I sank to the floor sobbing.

I lay in bed for three days. Not metaphorically. Literally.
I wailed. I screamed into pillows. My body couldn't contain the
grief. No one came. No flowers. No awkward hugs. Just my
husband, somewhere in the fog, telling my son, "Mom's just very
sad." Very sad. Like that even came close.

There was a giant hole in my chest. There still is. Micah
was the last person I let my guard down with.

I pride myself on hypervigilance—reading rooms,
catching energy shifts, noticing what others ignore. It's a trauma
skill. And it's served me well.

With Micah, I relaxed.
I thought he was okay.
I thought we were okay.

We'd had lunch the day before. Talked about everything
and nothing. I even asked—genuinely excited—if we'd be doing
our traditional dinner together, the one where we assigned roles.
His answer was vague. I didn't catch it. He walked out of my
office, held the door open, and said,

"At least we both always wanted what was best for kids."
That was the last thing he ever said to me.

I didn't see it.
I didn't see it.
That's what haunts me the most.

Eventually, I got out of bed.
Because I realized—in all my grief—that my students were hurting too.

I pulled myself together, put on real clothes, showed up to rehearsals, and tried to make space for their pain, even while I was still bleeding. I wasn't perfect for them. I was barely holding it together.

We changed the musical to *The Addams Family,* oddly light in its darkness, the perfect choice. Students and staff worked diligently to put on the show.

On closing night, no one said a word, but at curtain call, one by one, the students stepped forward and took off their shoes, placing them on the front of the stage.

Micah often didn't like to wear shoes.

It was their way of honoring him.

It was too much for me. Like the photos someone had quietly added to the set—images of him, tucked into corners for the final performance.

I cried the entire time I conducted the show. Quietly. Uncontrollably.

Why?

Because that's what real teachers do.
That's what survivors do.
That's what I do.

I don't know if I'll ever truly forgive myself for missing the signs, for not being the one he called, for believing, even briefly, that our friendship could protect him.

I've lost others since Micah—students, friends, even alumni—and each time it rattles me. It also reminds me why I stay.

As a survivor, I've had—and sometimes still have—to fight that darkness myself. I know how loud it can be. I know what it whispers. I do not make **that** choice.

How could he choose differently?
I will never understand.

Why do I stay?

So I can listen.
So I can notice.
So maybe, just maybe, someone else won't feel quite so alone.

I hope—I pray—that by holding space for others, some healing happened.

For them.
For me.
For whatever part of him might still be listening.

Chapter 16
The Hardest Choice

After Micah, I thought more than once about disappearing. I chose to stay because I've seen what that kind of absence does to the people left behind. There are nights when the question shows up like an old injury.

You realize the life you chose to feel safe in was never actually safe.

No safety in childhood.

No safety in the adult journey.

Not even in retirement—what you once hoped might feel like an afterlife.

Childhood broke my body.

Adulthood has tried to break my spirit.

And still, I stay.

Not because I'm weak. Not because I can't imagine another life. Not because I haven't thought about leaving this one altogether. I stay because I know what happens when someone doesn't.

After Micah died, I saw it all.

The wreckage.

The guilt.

The unanswered questions that shredded students and friends—people who loved him more than he ever knew.

I know what suicide does to the people left behind.

I will not do that to my children.
My grandchildren.
My husband.
My friends.
My former students who still text me, years later, because they believe I'm still worth listening to. I won't hand them the grief that others handed me.

My parents did that kind of damage.
Bad Behavior does that kind of damage.

But me?
No.

I survive. Not because I'm unbreakable—but because I refuse to become someone else's breaking point.

That's the hardest choice I make.
Over and over.
Every single day.

I stay.

Chapter 17
Letters from Bob

"I love you, mind, body, and soul. I need your presence as much as I need you." —Bob

I still don't have the right words. But I kept his. I still have the stack—real, physical letters. Pages and pages, folded and faded. The kind you hold in your hands and unfold like something sacred. They were written over four years by the young man who, I believe, truly loved me.

I was never someone's everything before—not in a good way. I was My Father's everything, but in a twisted, possessive, controlling way that had nothing to do with love. Before I met Bob, I didn't know unselfish love even existed.

Up to that point, love had looked like this:

A father who abused me with no conscience.

A mother who ignored what was going on in her house, while she read her books and went to church to sing in the choir.

A God who didn't answer my prayers, more like pleas, to take away the pain—My Father.

I didn't know someone could love you just because you were you. Not because they needed to own you, use you, or to get their iced tea—while I was practicing my music. Bob's letters were the first time I felt seen without being claimed for someone else's agenda.

Bob, my high school sweetheart, was my safe space in an otherwise unsafe world. He loved me with his whole heart, and he told me so—often, earnestly, and without apology.

He wrote about college, about being away from home, about life—but mostly, he wrote about his love for me. How much he missed me. What we would do when we were together. How I made him feel alive.

Bob didn't save me.
But he reminded me I was worth saving.
He's the reason I remembered what it felt like to be loved. There's a difference.

After the CT scan—and a radiologist using the word cancer—I was faced with what might be the end of my journey. How would that look? How would I walk that path and stay true to myself—and to the ones I loved? Not in a tragic, dramatic way. Just…practical. I had lived through too much already, and I wasn't sure I wanted to do it again. There would be no chemo. No losing myself.

But there would be:
Remembering what it felt like to be loved with someone's whole heart.
The kind of love—the quiet, steady kind—that leaves a mark. Even after he was gone. Even when life got harder. Even when I forgot what it felt like.
When you've spent most of your life surviving, it's hard to know what safe love really is. Harder still to believe you deserve it.
At that moment, I asked myself,
"Who do I love with MY whole heart?"

That very same day, I took my grandson to story time, like I did most Wednesdays. He wiggled, he giggled, he blew bubbles. He sang out *See You Later, Alligator* with his arms wide and a grin that could break your heart.

I watched him.

Right there, on that primary-colored carpet, surrounded by noise and laughter—and other squirmy three-year-olds—I had my answer:

I love him.
I love his siblings.
I love my children.
I love my husband.
I love my dear friends.

And I love all the children I have had the privilege to teach—every student who has ever come through my classroom door, sung in my choirs, learned secondary dominate chords, whispered secrets after class, cried after a solo audition, handed me notes folded into squares, or told me what their stepfather had done to them.

That's where my love went.
That is why I stayed.
That is why I'm still here.
That is why I'm writing this.

Because the love didn't disappear.
It multiplied.

And when I thought the story was over, my three-year-old grandson drummed an invisible drum kit in his Metallica shirt to Pirates of the Caribbean's *Seven Seas* in the back seat of my Buick.

I still have more chapters to write.

Chapter 18
Food for Thought

The one love language my mother had was cooking. Lasagna. Enchiladas. Fried chicken with mashed potatoes and gravy. Sounds delicious, right?

In my childhood, my mother cooked according to the 'Four Basic' food groups: milk, meat, fruits and vegetables, and bread and cereal—though that's technically five or even six? In 1958, at the height of the USDA's influence, she had been a home economics major. You had to do what the USDA said in 1960, according to Good Housekeeping and Perfect Wives. Especially Naval Officer's wives? Like she never broke a rule.

Married in three months to a divorced man with two abandoned kids. Exactly what sweet southern Baptist girls are supposed to do—or not. Anyway, this time, she followed the rules to the letter.

Every night, except Sundays, she'd have one of us girls—never my brother, of course—set the table with cloth napkins, folded the 'proper' way. The whole table was set up in the proper way: forks on the left, knife on the right with the blade facing in, then the spoon. I still set a table like this today. Muscle memory, I guess. Or maybe just proof that some patterns stick, whether we mean for them to or not.

At 5:00 p.m. sharp, the family would sit down, bow our heads, and pray. I never understood why. My Father didn't believe in God, and he certainly didn't pray. For my mother, prayer mostly served as a way to glance past 'sin.'

The family—minus My Father—would each take a polite portion from the 'four' food groups.

It sounds easy.

It wasn't.

Like everything else in my life. You had to estimate your portion in a way that felt satisfying, but not so satisfying that it might be criticized as fattening. Luckily, I could eat as much as I wanted back then. One of the only things I wish I could bring back from childhood.

That freedom.

That metabolism.

And then—every night—My Father took all the serving bowls and ceremoniously ate the rest of the food.

Directly from the bowls.

Every last bite.

Even my mother's mashed potatoes—my favorite.

Like it was his right.

Because he believed it was.

He controlled everything.

Except the night my mother made calves' liver with mushrooms. She had worked on it all afternoon. I was looking forward to the meal, because I'd watched the care she put into preparing it. I took love where I could get it.

We all sat down, bowed our heads, prayed—except My Father—and dug in. Or so I thought.

I was a 'good girl' at mealtime. I ate everything. Like closing your eyes and jumping—except I opened my mouth and swallowed. I'm pretty sure I fell in love with mushroom sauce that day. Finally, I looked up after eating half the meal. No one else was eating.

I was halfway through my plate. But that didn't matter. My Father stood up and said, "Let's go to McDonald's."

This wasn't a quick trip. Back then, McDonald's was a thirty-minute drive—before they existed on every street corner.

But you didn't question My Father. That could mean a backhanded slap. The family dutifully piled into the car, drove half around the island, and ordered Big Macs and Filet-O-Fish with french fries. The rest of the family was elated. I was full.

I learned that food would become my love language, not because my mother intentionally passed it down. But it was the only consistent nurturing she offered. And maybe only because it was required for a Girl Scout badge—she was the troop leader.

The summer before I left for college, I typed up a mix of my favorite recipes—many pulled from my mother's handwritten collection—on index cards labeled 'From the Kitchen of Sheryl.' I carefully filed each one into a little metal recipe box, decorated with green vines and yellow flowers—the decorative style of the 80s. I still have it, hidden in a cabinet. The corners are rusted now, the cards soft from years of handling. I don't use it much anymore, but it's one of the only things from that time that truly feels like it had *my* name on it.

I understood that food could fix almost everything. At least for men. I have three sons, three grandsons, and a husband who rarely go out to eat. Why should they if the food is better at home? My cooking has lured a cute college boy into my life with homemade lasagna. It can calm a crying child or make a hard day feel less hard.

Mother's milk is technically food, right? I 'cooked' that too. Nine years total—divided among four children. That's a lot of breastfeeding.

I nourished grumpy children, brought cheesy potatoes to hockey parties, cooked for my students and, in the process, found out that teenagers don't care how fancy your meal is—only that someone made it.

At my retirement concert, one former student stood in front of a full auditorium. I was expecting a story about music or friendship, but it turned out to be something else. The story he chose to recall? It was about food. More specifically, feeding him.

He explained to the crowd that he came into my office after a horrible day and, before he could even sit down, I handed him a cheese stick and a bottle of water. That's all it took. He said it changed everything. *Teachers, take note: always have emergency cheese sticks.*

I cook a *Hawai'i* favorite, chili and rice, on rainy nights when my grown children come home and need comfort food. I invite students over for backyard dinners with homemade chicken teriyaki on the grill and sticky white rice—not exactly a midwestern standard. I cook for my friend on the Fourth of July—at HER house. I bring homemade potato soup to the 'other side' of the family when we're forced into the same house by impending loss. Are you salivating yet?

I've even prepared Pinterest-worthy charcuterie boards—when I was invited next door. Yeah, I got invited. Not much since. Maybe it is my dark humor. Or maybe it was the fact that they just don't get me. Either way... Eventually, I found a better solution for dinner time: meal kits.

I finally gave up deciding what to cook, writing grocery lists, driving to the store, putting items in a cart, taking them out again, bagging them, loading the car, unloading the car, and restocking my fridge—*all* of it. I surrendered.

To be honest, I've tried two food kit companies because when one lets me down—like with late deliveries or missing ingredients—I switch to the other. Sometimes I need both at once for a big gathering. Or a holiday. Or when I'm just too tired to make another decision. I've ordered over 1,300 boxes to date. Yes, that's a lot of boxes.

I'm not just eating anymore. I've found joy in preparing the meal, whether for the whole family or just for myself. It's a tangible, repetitive strategy that calms my soul.

At the end of a long day, I pick a recipe card from the kit, open the brown paper bag, and spread everything out on the counter. I chop. I stir. I follow instructions. And when I'm done, I have a meal I can share. A meal I can enjoy. Tasty, filling, and good for my compromised body.

And while I savor the preparing, the serving, the eating.

No one tells me what the portions should be.
No one takes the serving bowl away.
No one is saying we're going to McDonald's instead.

Just a recipe.
A plan.
A meal to share.
I build one dinner at a time.

Life is not that simple.
At least dinner comes with instructions and an endgame.

Chapter 19
The First Brick I Chose

Going to college was always my endgame through childhood. I could leave—'leaving on a jet plane.' I needed a place to escape to and launch from. Funny thing is, I never thought past that plane. The plan began and ended with getting to college.

Most kids think about majors, careers, roommates, living on their own, or the parties they're going to enjoy. Trust me—I've graduated thousands of university-bound students. But for me? College meant one thing: getting far away from My Father *as soon as possible.*

I barely knew what it took to get into a 'mainland' college—one that would put an ocean between me and my parents. Not like the seniors today with their counselors and overpriced tutors. As usual, there was little guidance. Not from my parents. Not from my voice teacher. And, of course, not even from my choir teacher. Yet I knew one thing for sure: staying wasn't going to be part of my future.

My journey into music school would happen from thousands of miles away. Remember, this was before FaceTime. Before high-def recordings on a fancy iPhone. Before you could hire someone to polish your audition tape and make you sound good.

There were no discount airline tickets. Even if there had been, My Father would NEVER have let me hop on a plane for something so frivolous as music.

I had a voice.
And music.

It had become more than something I was good at. It was how I managed to hold myself together. When the opportunity came to attend a summer camp held on the campus of Baylor University, I found a way to visit.

The strange part? It wasn't even a music camp. It was FCA—Fellowship of Christian Athletes. Funny thing: My father approved it because he thought it was a sports camp. I'd never been on a sports team in my life. Not even close. I went anyway. There I was, singing worship songs in the evenings and pretending I wasn't completely out of place.

The university quad was a paved courtyard encircled by striking red-brick, castle-like buildings with steeply pitched roofs and ornate white cupolas, designed in a late 19th-century collegiate Gothic style. The campus sparkled. I always imagined *menehune*, *Hawai'ian* leprechauns, coming out at night to trim the bushes and polish the sidewalks. It was majestic and reverent all at the same time.

I managed to set up an interview with the head of the vocal music department. I walked into this awe-inspiring building and was convinced this was where I wanted to go to school—to escape.

I met Dr. Robert Young. A gentle, elderly man with a calm, loving demeanor. He greeted me with warmth and kindness. He showed me into his office, filled with music scores and a well-loved grand piano. We made small talk for a moment, and then he asked if I had REALLY come all the way from *Hawai'i*—3,778 miles away.

I nodded. His face lit up. He told me he'd been stationed at Pearl Harbor during World War II. He paused. Looked down, as if in a memory, and declared he would love for me to be part of the Baylor family. He would teach me and be my cheerleader.

Strangely enough, he never heard me sing that day. He never asked for my transcripts or my application—which, to be fair, were pretty bad and mostly nonexistent.

I was from *Hawai'i*, after all.

I felt valued. I felt safe. Someone believed in me. Someone who loved music and the *Hawai'ian* culture as much as I did—and who recognized that I belonged. I was determined to work toward attending his school. And a year later, I did.

My mother sewed—one of the skills she learned from her Home Economics college major—a full 'mainland' wardrobe for me. Beautiful wool skirts and long-sleeved button-downs with thin satin ribbons added to tie at the collar. Not exactly practical for *Hawai'i*, but definitely stylish for Texas.

I packed everything into a gigantic trunk with the same small, breakable lock as my diary. At church, the congregation sang *Aloha 'Oe*. Church members draped my neck in leis. My Father cried—and cried—and cried. I don't remember my mother ever crying. I certainly didn't cry. There were no regrets.

I boarded the plane, my heart strangely steady. This was long before TSA, when loved ones could walk you right to the gate. My Father was standing at the gate, handkerchief in hand, dabbing at his tears.

As we flew over the lights of *Waikiki*, I pressed my forehead to the window and quietly heard the lyrics in my head:

Each time Honolulu city lights
Stir up memories in me
Each night Honolulu city lights
Bring me back again

I loved *Hawai'i*. I would come back—but not as the same girl. Not with the same trauma.

A lot happened at Baylor—good, bad, and ugly. I'm going to make a choice and tell you the good.

I told someone about life before college.

My Father. The abuse.

And they listened.

He listened.

He did something.

They did something.

113

I don't even remember exactly when or how I told him. Maybe that's not the part that matters. What I remember is how he looked at me.

Not with shock.
Just…'presence.'

And somehow, he told the school authorities. I don't know how it happened, but the university didn't ignore me. They set up free counseling. They watched out for me. They saw me. That was already more than I'd ever had. It didn't stop there.

Spring break was coming and I was expected to go home. Before I left, the university's provost called me into his office. Was I in trouble? I certainly wasn't being summoned because I was the best student. Or the best singer. Or the best Christian. The only other time I'd ever stepped foot in that building was to pay a bill. Did I owe money? Were they about to collect? I sat down.

He looked at me gently and said, "We've heard your story. We know you're afraid to go home." Then he told me something that changed everything, "Baylor University will stand behind you. You have a place to come back to. No matter what happens, we will see to it that you graduate."

That gave me something I had never been given before: Permission to imagine not just surviving, but thriving. That was quite a new feeling—a new experience. Thank you, Baylor.

As I sat down with my new counselor, he shared something I didn't want to hear—but couldn't ignore: Abuse like this rarely stops with just one child.

No!
Lord, no!
My sister, my brother?

I had tried to protect my sister, sixteen months younger than me. I thought I had. I wanted to believe my mother had too—but maybe she hadn't.

I would go back and find out. What was going to happen? Was my sister abused, too? Would My Father give up on 'his project'? Or would he double down?

Spoiler alert: he doubled down.

When I returned home, it was like I'd never left.

Except I had.
I was different.

The day I arrived I drove my sister to basketball practice and steeled myself. It is the only time I have ever truly talked to her about this. I don't know why. Maybe I am a coward, but not that day.

I blurted it out,
"Has Dad ever touched you?"

And the answer sent my body into high alert.
"Yes," is all she said, looking out the window of the car.

My mind was screaming "NOOOOO," but I managed to mumble,
"I'll stop it. TODAY! I PROMISE!"

That night, I stood in my room and knew I had to do something. I didn't have a plan. I just knew he wasn't going to touch me—or my sister—again.

I found a baseball bat and placed it strategically in my room. I had never picked up a bat in my life, let alone swung one. Hadn't I watched carefully on TV when a batter clenched the bat and wiggled his fingers just right? It didn't look hard. I didn't know how to use it, but I knew I would.

The door creaked.
I was ready.

When he entered my room in the middle of the night, I jumped out of bed, grabbed the bat, closed my eyes, and swung.
I missed.
It didn't matter.
It was a powerful message:
You will not touch me.
You will not touch my sister.

He stepped back. And then…

He started talking.
One of 'those' talks.
About how he loved me.
About how what he wanted was somehow right.

I didn't care what he had to say. I just wanted him out. I had promised her it would stop. And that night, I kept my promise. I swung again. Harder. And again. Missing, but with conviction. Until he finally left—fuming, red-faced, and furious. There were consequences to be paid. Of course, as usual, consequences for everyone around me.

He punished me.
He punished my mother.

The next day, after he took away my airline ticket and announced that I would not be returning to school, my mother came to me—so predictable.
She begged, "If you're just a 'good girl'", everything will be all right, and you can go back to school."
This time, with people and Baylor behind me, I repeated over and over, looking down, away from my mother, "No. I can't. And I won't."

She FINALLY asked the question. The question I had been waiting eighteen years to hear. "Did your father touch you?" I was stunned. Something clicked, or the consequences were too much for her to bear. She had asked. I nodded yes.

Could it be that when faced with consequences herself, my mother finally asked the question? I had wanted to believe she didn't know. I convinced myself for years that she didn't.

What happened next is my mother's story—not mine to tell. Yet I can tell you this:
> It wasn't "Let's leave."
> It wasn't "Oh my God."
> It wasn't safe.
> It wasn't clear.

My Father came to me the next morning and declared:
He would not touch me again.
> No apology.
> No explanation.
> Just that—flat and final.

He handed me back the airline ticket.

We all packed into the car and drove to our family's 'celebration restaurant,' Pearl City Taverns, with live monkeys behind a glass cage. Were we supposed to celebrate something? Wasn't he supposed to get arrested or something? Lobster for dinner?
> Symbolic?
> Probably.
> Hindsight.
> Should I have let the monkeys out?
> Definitely.
> That was that.

I was put on a plane and sent back to school. I hoped my siblings were safe, now that my mother had finally asked the question.

I was surviving.

I never would've had the courage—even as a Leo born in the Year of the Tiger—to take on that project without Baylor University's backing.

Looking back, it wasn't how it was supposed to go down. The story didn't end.

It was just the beginning.

Chapter 20
Touching Dirt

Gardening and yard work—two very different tasks—were never things I imagined I'd do as a child or adult.

My Father demanded that anything to do in the yard was "men's work" although, truthfully, I never saw him do a thing around the house. Even when my parents had very little money, there was always some for hired help—for the house, the yard, and for whatever My Father and mother didn't want to do themselves. Yard work wasn't exactly "man's work." It was help's work.

As an adult, I mow the lawn. I weed. I plant pots of flowers. I tend my plants. Sometimes the outside of my home is beautiful. Sometimes it's a mess. Sometimes life gets in the way:

Trips to Monte Carlo.

Suspicious nodules on a lung scan.

A mother-in-law who slowly dies.

Sometimes the flowers bloom. Sometimes they wither. Sometimes the deer eat them. Sometimes I keep the weeds out. Sometimes I don't. But I touch the dirt. I dig. I tend. And that's the difference.

Gardens and lawns must be tended consistently, or they will do one of two things: either get taken over by native plants—I call them weeds—or die.

Much like people.

I vaguely remember our yard in California, where Kelly used to run. It was fenced in, and there was a flower bed in the corner that someone clearly cared for.

The first house we lived in on *O'ahu* had a small front lawn and a backyard that looked like a place children might play.

Like the inside of our house—and like our family—it was only beautiful from the outside. The lawn was a special Japanese grass that looked lush, but it was prickly. So prickly that it hurt to touch it.

The last childhood house—the one My Father sold to a friend, who sold it back to his third wife—sat on a double lot. Tiered into three levels, thick hedges lining the property on either side, and rows of banana trees. So many I still don't like to eat bananas. Outside my bedroom window stood a giant plumeria tree. The scent filled my room through the open louvers. It was beautiful to look at but, like everything else in my life, it had a sticky residue that was difficult to get off my fingers.

I rarely went into the yard. Because it was *my* house. A house, what *you* might call your home, was a place for me to stay away from—at all costs. It was never lost on me that when I was at the house, there was always one place I was expected to be:

With My Father.

To be seen.

To be possessed.

In ninth grade, I was desperate for extra credit in biology. I approached my teacher—hair a little greasy, probably from working in her own yard—and asked what I could do to earn some points. She told me to come after school.

When I arrived, she gave me a hand shovel and gestured to the dirt patch right in front of her classroom. A little rectangle of earth, maybe three feet by one, surrounded by a cement 'hallway.' Every classroom had one, but only the biology teacher noticed.

"Clear out all the weeds," she said.

I wasn't sure why she chose that task for me, but I got to work. For over an hour, I dug every weed out of that box, then moved on to the next one in front of the marine biology classroom. I need to point out that if I had just done my homework, I wouldn't have needed to dig in the dirt.

When I handed the shovel back, she looked me directly in the eye and said,

"I didn't think you'd do it."

"Do what?" I asked.

"Touch the dirt," she said.

I was surprised.

She had pegged me as a Miss Priss—too good to 'touch something dirty.' It occurred to me in that moment that she had given me that task, expecting me to refuse. I didn't. I was tending my own garden.

I guess you can't judge a book by its cover. Nor can you look at brick pieces scattered across the floor and know exactly what they'll become.

It's not a punishment.
It's not even a task.
It's an opportunity.
To clear the ground.
To dig in the dirt.

Before anything new can grow, you have to clear the weeds and feel the soil beneath your fingers. That's where the real work begins.

Sometimes, tending the garden is the bravest thing we do.

Measure 4
Legacy, Voice, and Meaning

Chapter 21
Of Water and Fire

I am drawn to water and fire.
I am of water and fire.

In so many traditions, these two elements are opposites—destruction and healing, rage and surrender. I grew up on an island surrounded by one and formed by the other. Volcanoes made my home, and the ocean kept it alive. Fire burns until it touches water—and when it does, new land is born. That's how you make something new—from what seems like ruin.

Fireplaces are uncommon in *Hawai'i*—probably because it never gets cold, like midwestern cold. I insisted on 'real' fireplaces in every house I purchased. Real fire. Not the fake lightbulb-in-a-box kind. I got lucky. My home has two fireplaces, along with an additional fire pit on the back deck that matches my furniture—if it works. Spiders love it as much as I do. They build webs right where I'm trying to light the flame.

Sometimes I sit out on the porch close to the fire pit, alone, letting the flames warm my knees while I try to let go of whatever the day burned through.

From far away, I still watch as *Pele*, the *Hawai'ian* goddess of fire, sends lava flowing from *Kīlauea's* crater—creating more land, more *Hawai'i*.

On my last visit, I walked on the barren lava field—jagged and ancient—and saw a group of rocks, formed from a fissure years before. You're going to think I'm *pūpule* but, as I stood there, feeling no wind, no movement, shapes shifted, and I saw four ancient *kūpuna,* towering above me.

"Save the *keikis,*" they were screaming. "They are crying, and no one is listening. Save the children, don't let your voice be silenced," the *kūpuna* begged.

It was random.
Unexpected.
Powerful.

As I looked down into a small fissure, a tiny purple flower blossomed, thriving in the barren rocks. That moment on the lava—surrounded by silence and ancestors—reminded me of something fundamental, from destruction comes new growth. It's a cycle I've learned to trust.

Water always calls me back. As a *keiki,* water was the only safe place I had. I was never touched in the bathroom. Never cornered by the pool. Never.

No matter how cold the water, how loud the wind, or how dark the sky, if I needed safety, I found it in water. Maybe that's why I am never afraid to fly over the ocean. Only land. Strange, right?

When I am drowning in something too big to name, I go to the water. When I have one of those massive cluster migraines—a lovely gift of trauma—I crawl under the shower and let hot water trickle down my head until it runs out. Although now I have a tankless water heater. Problem solved. Hot water on demand.

When the pain down under is unbearable or my restless legs keeps me from sleeping, I fill the tub with the hottest water I can stand and soak the pain away.

Off *Oʻahu's* North Shore, at the end of the court battle with My Father, my Husband and I stayed at a studio cottage right on the beach. During the day, I played in the ocean with a teenage *honu*, sea turtle. At night, I floated in the waves for hours—obviously forgetting about the sharks.

The ocean washed the ugly away.

In those hours, I remembered who I was—not the fighter, not the teacher, not the wife—but the girl who was safe in water.

During the Monte Carlo cruise with my mother—in the month of May, not exactly warm—I jumped into the Mediterranean off the back of the boat. The crew watched in disbelief as a woman over 60 swam alone, staying in the cold water for hours, day after day. To be fair, most of them were from the South Pacific, and knew they did not want to be in cold water to save this old woman. Each day, more staff members gathered to watch the *kupuna*—I prefer that word—who just had to be in the water. Dolphins played nearby, adding to the magic. I emerged from that water, soaked, freezing, and alive.

I've passed my love for water down without even meaning to. When my children were little and sick, I threw them into the shower or a warm bath without hesitation. I have proof: the handle of the guest shower cracked when my 200-pound teenager, suffering from migraines, leaned on it until it broke. It took ten years for me to finally fix it.

My son now does the same with his kids. They inherited the migraines, too. Generational trauma—so generous. I would have preferred to pass down kindness and empathy. Oh well—I tried.

I'm not sure the outcomes were technically 'medicinal,' but my mother's instinct said, "Do it." Let the water hit their backs. Let it wash the fever, the ache, or the tantrum away.

And if I can't be in the water, I want to be near it.

Each morning—rain, shine, storm, or calm—I wake to look out my windows at a pond, often catching the sunrise over the trees. Herons, swans, ducks, and those darn messy geese gather there—each drawn to the water's edge, each finding life.

In the winter the pond freezes, and snow accumulates on top. Snow is water, too, scientifically speaking. Snow was something I never experienced until college. Only the Big Island of *Hawai'i* has snow on the peaks of *Mauna Kea* and *Mauna Loa*.

During my first year at Baylor, in Texas, a light dusting of snow shut down campus, sending my blue Ford Mustang gently skidding at two miles an hour. The lesson I learned quickly was to turn into the skid, not away. I deeply appreciated the traffic sign for stopping the car without a dent. Driving in snow is not something that is taught in *Hawai'i* state driver's education. Come to think of it, I never took driver's education.

THIS STORY IS TOO GOOD TO PASS…

When I was nine, My Father took me to the golf course for my birthday. Not my idea of a happy birthday—but My 'Father Knows Best.' Can you see the half smile emoji in your head?

He plopped me into the driver's seat of a golf cart and said, "Go." That was my driver's education.

Fast forward to fourteen—again, on my birthday. My mom took me to get my official driver's license. Back then, you could test at fourteen with no formal training. The clerk asked to see my mom's license.

Expired.

So, my mom called My Father. Can you imagine what happened? His was expired, too. He had to take the written and driving tests right there in the DMV.

Eventually, my mom's best friend—the one who found Honey at the airfield—showed up with a valid license so I could take the test.

Guess what?

I failed.

Don't be disappointed.

That night I drove the course again and again, determined not to cross over the solid line between lights when turning left—as I'd been told. You guessed it: I failed because I was doing exactly what I was told. So much for "be a 'good girl'" and doing what I was told.

I came back the next day.

Passed.

Because that's what I do. I figure things out. Eventually. Even if it means circling the same road a hundred times first.

Maybe that's why I don't just survive winter—I love it. Yes—shocker—girl from *Hawai'i* loves snow.

Like persistence, snow has its own rhythm. It covers everything, softens sharp edges, and forces the world to slow down, to take a breath.

When winter drops the temperature low enough, my Husband transforms the frozen pond into a giant neighborhood ice rink. He spends hours clearing snow, flooding the surface, and aiming the truck headlights across the ice for a late-night skate. Adults, kids, and even dogs wander over with chairs, coolers, and hockey nets—turning the frozen pond into an instant neighborhood party, laughter slicing through the crisp air. I see the joy he finds in creating this shared magic—an oasis of community and fun in the cold. For me, it's a quiet testament to his generosity and care.

Everyone skates, or at least tries to. My boys, men now, skate gracefully, masterfully handling the hockey puck and shooting past their beginner father. My grandchildren clutch homemade PVC pipe sleds for stability. Even Rusty the DOG races across the ice with glee, sliding to greet the other dogs in the neighborhood.

I don't skate. I fall—often. I once executed a beautiful swan dive—right on my side. The next-door neighbor—the doctor— asked, yelling from across the ice, if I was alright and needed help getting up. I just sat there on the cold ice, smiled, and said I was fine.

Because that is what survivors do.

When I finally got up—alone—I discovered I had fractured my fourth rib.

It's definitely okay that I don't skate. I'm really here for the snow—the kind that sticks and piles high. Snow that blankets trees, streets, and rooftops. Snow you can roll into a snowman with your grandchildren. Snow that provides a clean slate—a quiet moment—if only for an instant.

But ice and snow aren't the only forces that shaped me. There's also fire—hot, mesmerizing flames. Especially lava. It is dangerous, but I also know what happens when it meets the sea. I've seen the steam rise. I've stood on the beautiful black and green sand it leaves behind.

That's the point.

Water doesn't just wash things away. Sometimes it makes room for something new.

Fire and water—one scorches, the other soothes. Together they've forged who I am.

Chapter 22
HONU

Honu is the *Hawai'ian* word for sea turtle. I bet you think you can understand half the words spoken on the series *Chief of War* by now.

Growing up, I never encountered a *honu*—not once, not on land, not in the ocean. I ignored turtles. They weren't pretty, clever, or cuddly. In fact, in the fifth grade, we were asked to identify an animal that represented ourselves. I chose the tiger. They had claws to protect themselves. Fitting. Little did I know, I was born in the Chinese Year of the Tiger.

Honu is believed to embody wisdom and patience—two qualities I have needed more than I ever expected. The time came when, once again, I shut my eyes, stepped off, and jumped. I could no longer stay quiet. I was willing to fight for other survivors like me. I didn't know where that road would go, only that I needed to try.

Three years before I jumped, my *pūpule*, lovable, brother came to visit the mainland after years of homelessness and time in the state mental hospital. The visit to my home was supposed to be a reward. A reunion. A fresh start.

Instead, I got a phone call from the pilot of the plane that flew to my home state. Yes, the *pilot*.

"Is RC your brother?" he asked.

Oh boy. Here we go again.

"He seems a little off." A little? You think?

"Is anyone meeting him at the airport?" the pilot asked.

Luckily, my calm and collected Husband was already there, chasing through the baggage claim, trying to find RC. He quickly whisked my brother away from the pilot and any other victims of his antics.

When my Husband got him home it was late. At least they were safe. Did my brother greet me with a hug? Get settled in his room? Nope, his first order of business was to demand a steak dinner. Seriously? Right now?

By the way, we don't even eat steak, so it's not like one was waiting in the freezer. And besides, McDonald's was more in our budget. He got a hamburger—and he was not happy.

The next day, in a full manic state, my brother had completely redecorated my house. And by 'redecorated,' I mean he hid all my home décor. Everything. He hadn't slept in 48 hours.

The local police came to assess his mental status. Thankfully, they knew me from my position at the high school. I'd worked with them for years through school events and community performances. Let's just say, I was a bit of a local celebrity—as much as a high school choir teacher can be.

When they assessed the situation, they gave my brother a choice: they could take him to the hospital, or his sister could.

What did my brother pick?
He chose his sister.

My Husband and I drove him to the nearest hospital. They released him almost immediately. We then dropped him off at the crisis center. He was soon admitted to the local mental health hospital and graduated to lockdown within the hour.

Somehow, he'd ended up with Medicaid coverage in *two* states—because, of course, that's completely fine and never raises any red flags. *Surprise: It does.*

Long story short: He was supposed to be extradited back to *Hawai'i* OR I could break him out of lockdown myself and fly him home.

There was a small issue—truthfully, probably many—but this was the big one. I hadn't been on a plane in 25 years. I hadn't been back to *Hawai'i* in 25 years. So, naturally, my first flight across the Pacific in two and a half decades would be with my manic bi-polar brother.

What did I choose?
I got on the plane.

RC and I sat in the very back row— you know, the one where the chairs don't recline? I definitely don't do that anymore. The only reason we made it through the ten hours in the air was that the flight attendant constantly fed him. I racked up $200 of sandwiches and Coke. Tell me that doesn't scream manic.

There was a really nice guy sitting in the aisle seat who sort of locked us in. Looking back, I'm pretty sure he was strategically planted there by the airline—specifically for us. I was having the time of my life—NOT.

We finally landed in *Hawai'i* and, naturally, our first stop was the State Mental Hospital. Because nothing says 'Welcome home' quite like that. Of course, I had rented a red Corvette convertible. I needed *something* fun, and RC loved going fast. So we pulled up in style.

Inside, the psychiatric team met me in the lobby. The social worker had never laid eyes on me but sat down on a couch—that had seen better days—and talked like we were old friends. After a little small talk about the flight and the weather, he leaned in gently and said, "I know your story."

Which one?
The one where my brother hid all my decor?
The one where my son had a tumor?
Oh.
That one.
Sexual abuse.

Then he handed me a business card with a lawyer's contact information. He explained there was a movement in *Hawai'i* to extend the statute of limitations for civil cases involving childhood sexual abuse. I could sue My Father. I could help set a precedent for other survivors.

A new, quiet law had created a two-year window for such civil cases. It was open. For me.

For years My Father denied it all—brushed off anyone who dared to suggest something was wrong. But this time? He actually bragged to my brother's psychiatric team about grooming me. 'Who's popular now?'

My Father bragged to the team about his instrumental role in my success in life. Told them that because of his 'relationship' with me, I had grown into an exceptional woman. That's debatable.

I didn't know about that legal window. Hardly anyone did. That was intentional.

I had always daydreamed about suing My Father someday—imagining I had time—not realizing I only had eighteen months after turning eighteen to take action. Like so many survivors, I thought justice would be waiting when I was finally ready. That simply wasn't true in *Hawai'i*. That's simply not true in more states than I can count.

It took me months to muster the courage to pick up the phone and call that number. Years to step into a courtroom. And a parade of lawyers and judges before the case was finally 'settled.'

I didn't want to settle.
I wanted a trial.
I wanted the truth dragged into the light.
Into every ugly corner.
I wanted to embarrass My Father.

Burn the whole circus down—with his lies in the center ring. I wanted to set a precedent. To say, "This happened. It matters. We don't keep quiet anymore."

Challenges would come during the next five years. The psychiatric team—where I got the business card—wouldn't testify. The original high-profile lawyer didn't believe me. He threw my case to a junior associate who simply wanted his 33% cut plus taxes. I'm not sure he believed me either.

I AM getting to the *Honu*.

After years of showing up. Putting my life on hold. On display. I flew to *Hawai'i* for a court hearing. The clerk at the desk looked surprised—shocked— that I'd flown in from the mainland for a court hearing.

Who does that?
ME.

A new judge had been appointed. My new lawyer didn't show up. Meanwhile, My Father—representing himself—was allowed to walk back to the judge's chamber and speak privately with him while I sat silently in an empty courtroom. No representation. Traveling 4,000 miles—not in the back row this time—for nothing. It was a Monday. Pouring rain. Buckets of it.

A new bill to eliminate the statute of limitations had stalled in committee, caught up in politics and backroom deals. Or maybe it was that underground organization—the one My Father told me about—pulling strings behind the scenes. Either way, progress had ground to a frustrating halt. UGH!

My dearest friend was a constant presence since childhood—always gracious and supportive—even in the quiet moments when words were few. She suggested we drive to my favorite spot: the ocean, the water, my safe place. She knew exactly what I needed at that moment.

We drove through the storm, winding between the island's mountain ranges in her 2000 BMW Z3 sports car, barely able to see through the windshield. "Maybe it will be beautiful on the other side, at the North Shore," she said, breaking the silence. I agreed. Still—the rain kept coming.

As we approached Sunset Beach, I noticed a small dirt patch—the same spot where I used to park as a teenager to watch my high school sweetheart, Bob, surf. It had always been my safe place. Now the beach was empty, the sky dark, and the rain still falling.

What happened next may sound like fiction. My petite, impeccably dressed friend stood right there on the beach—a designer purse over her head—watching, dumbfounded. I entered my ocean. Letting waves wash away what my grandma used to call 'the ugly.'

As I swam out past the surf break, I saw a large shadow moving near me. My first thought: Crap. A hammerhead shark. Just like the ones I'd seen as a teen. I braced to punch it in the nose. But it wasn't a shark. It was a giant sea turtle. A *Honu*.

I had never seen one up close before. He was so close I could see the three stripes across his face, the markings on his long, powerful flippers. His shell was massive—wider than my arms could reach—and looked like a sculpture of tiny volcanoes, uneven and ancient. His eyes were round and green.

He looked straight at me.

He didn't look away.

He held my gaze until I broke it.

That would have been enough, to see such a majestic creature, and be seen. But it wasn't enough for him. Or her. It stayed with me. Followed me as I swam. Back and forth. For forty-five minutes. Always just a few feet away. I looked to shore. My friend was still there—standing in the rain, purse still on her head—watching.

And in that moment I realized my friend wouldn't abandon me. She would stand there—soaked to the bone; ruined designer bag—just to make sure I was okay.

I began swimming back to shore.
The *Honu* followed.

As I reached the waves and walked out of the water, the giant, ancient *Honu* swam with me. I turned back one last time from the shore. In the wave an arm's length away, he lifted his head above the surface and looked me straight in the eyes.

I heard it.
"It will be alright."
Then he disappeared into the sea.

That day changed something in me. Even now, I can feel the ancient *Honu*'s spirit beside me. It wouldn't be my last encounter. *Honu* have appeared often since—always with a message:
>**You will be okay.**
>**You will survive.**

I wear a *honu* on the inside of my right wrist.
To remind me of that day.

To remind me to:
Be Wise.
Be Patient.
And Endure.

To keep swimming, even when the current is strong.

Chapter 23
Symphony Angel

Some kids find comfort at home. I found it by staying busy. A strategy that's carried me through most of my life.

I filled every spare minute with something—anything—to stay away from my parents' house, My Father, and the chance I might be left alone with him.

I once read a book about reiki, a Japanese healing practice. What struck me was how it took this simple strategy—busy hands, happy heart—and ran with it.

I could have written that theory myself. Without even realizing it, I was already practicing it as a kid. Making music. Cooking. Swimming—not the swim-team kind. Decorating. Gardening. And a little, I said a little, homework.

As a teenager, I took piano, flute, and voice lessons. Worked at Liberty House—now a Macy's. Sold Avon. Played tennis. Danced ballet and jazz. Sang in every choir I could find—school, church, state. I snuck away to the beach whenever I could—not part of my father's plan. I might get sunburned and ruin my porcelain skin. What sixteen-year-old cared?

I was even a finalist for *Hawai'i* Junior Miss Contest—although my choice of talent number, *I'm Gonna Wash That Man Right Out of My Hair,* may have tanked it. I actually got my hair wet. Onstage. In front of a thousand people. Again, a little guidance might've helped.

But the truth was, I stayed busy so I could stay safe. Or at least during the day.

My high school friends described me as a sweet, smart girl who 'floated' down those long outdoor hallways. That's what they saw—because that's what I wanted them to see. I needed them to see.

Someone saw beyond that. Someone saw that I loved music. Someone knew it could be a lifeline. Someone anonymous knew they could give me something I needed.

My Symphony Angel.

An anonymous donor gifted season-long Honolulu Symphony tickets—second row seats at the Blaisdell Center—to deserving students.

Funny thing: every time I received two tickets, my mother took the second one and 'accompanied me.' Surprise! A cute boy by my side would have been much more fun.

I still don't know who donated the tickets. But the gift changed me.

It was the first time I sat in a velvet seat and heard a full orchestra live. The first time I saw that kind of power and precision up close—Dvořák's *New World Symphony*, Tchaikovsky's *Overture of 1812*, and Beethoven's *Ninth Symphony—Ode to Joy*. It changed how I listened. It certainly wasn't my parents' 007 records.

It gave me hope.
It gave me heart.

My favorite? The performance I'll never forget? Beverly Sills. She owned that stage. Every note she sang said, "I am here. I am seen." And in that moment, I knew what I wanted. I wanted to be heard.

Mahalo, Symphony Angel.

Chapter 24
Decorating

Somewhere along the way, projects—whether big or small—have become essential to me. A concert. A room. A person. Cooking. Raising pets. Raising kids.

It turns out this has a name. My counselor calls it compartmentalization. I am a master at it.

As a child, I had many projects—not yet mastered or finished—like the embroidery in my after-school enrichment class. I stitched through one flower instead of the whole bouquet. I am much better at completing my projects now.

I have always enjoyed decorating, even before HGTV. I love creating beautiful, comfortable spaces. Safe spaces—go figure. I made my childhood room special with my version of a dressing table tucked inside my closet. Maybe so I could hide?

When I arrived at Baylor University my freshman year, I showed up three days early to meet my roommate and decorate our dorm room. We headed to Sears—never my kind of store (roommate alert)—to buy matching bedspreads. They were yellow and brown. Joanna Gaines would be appalled. Not the last battle I lost with that roommate.

I decorated my home, my classrooms, and even my friends' homes—free of course. I used gifts, discarded treasures from the curb, old throw-away decor from the Salvation Army, and even Kai's building block models. All before it was popular for YouTube influencers to make a living out of spray paint and hot glue.

Time moved on, but my obsession with decorating didn't. Which means, of course, I was always decorating.

When I found out the nodules in my lungs could be a problem, everything shifted. A routine check suddenly wasn't routine at all. What did I do? Started a project, of course. The guest suite got volunteered—the upstairs one, close to the chaos. Because nothing says *coping strategy* like new curtains.

I wanted a space where, when my time came, I could feel safe. At home. Not alone—I know it sounds morbid.

After many of my surgeries; foot, female, heart, or COVID—technically not surgery but being quarantined twice for ten days is no picnic in the park—I was always sent to the master suite in the basement. Let's establish now that it's a very nice wing of the house and has a bathroom bigger than a racquetball court—yet I felt alone. Isolated.

During one bout of COVID over Thanksgiving, I was confined in the master suite with my very own Keurig and a pile of tea bags—complete with a walk-in closet larger than most ranch houses. Don't worry, I stuffed it with everything a sixty-something woman could use to become a Pinterest influencer.

Visitors, whom I had invited before I was dangerously contagious, came from out of town, and the party started—without me—in my house.

While the family gathered over turkey and fixings, my son came to the window in the downstairs suite, with my grandson, holding up a bottle of wine like a peace offering. Then he just walked away. He couldn't understand why I was upset. Was it the wine? Or the grandson?

If I were at my weakest, I'd want a space where I felt safe at home, where I felt seen and heard. I don't want to be alone in a room decorated with a homemade headboard, used curtains, and furniture that My Father had gifted.

The downstairs—well, technically two steps from the higher floor—bedroom has a big picture window. But it is so fogged up with condensation between the panes that it's hard to see the deer munching on all my flowers and the cat next door using my yard for his personal litter box.

I wanted, no, needed, a space that told me, "You are worth something." But healing doesn't always come through plans. Sometimes it starts with a quilt.

Right before retirement, I took my choir students to *Hawai'i*. It had been a dream for years, to share my culture and music with my incredibly special students.

Unfortunately, their parents—who tagged along—weren't so special and made the trip more difficult. The parents refused to follow the rules, feeling entitled, and personifying very 'bad behavior.' I was triggered.

I ducked into a hut at the Polynesian Cultural Center to breathe. Inside, *Hawai'ian* quilts hung on every wall. A *kupuna* Mormon woman sat carefully stitching one, just as I had once done with my grandma so long ago. As I exited through the back, I saw a quilt in ocean blue hanging on the outside wall, a *honu* pattern carefully stitched through it.

I found the price tag. Sticker shock. The ones at the swap meet were a fourth of the cost but not stitched lovingly in this hut. Like the ancient *Honu* in the ocean, these *honus* were calling to me. What did I do next? You guessed it. I bought the quilt.

I plopped my American Express on the counter—my go-to for racking up Delta miles—and pointed to the quilt. Instead of taking down the one I'd picked, the woman—I wish I wasn't focusing on the triggering parents—showed me the *honu* on the new quilt and quickly boxed it up for the trip to my mainland home.

As I anxiously waited for the box to arrive through UPS, I designed my new project around the quilt. Wallpaper. Rugs. Sheets. Lighting. All centered around this symbolic quilt—this piece, lovingly stitched by the Aunties, that meant something to me.

When I finished painting the room, including paint from head to a bruised toe, I furnished and cleaned it. I opened the box, took the quilt out, spread it on the bed, and noticed a label in the corner. MADE IN THE PHILIPPINES.

I looked twice. This wasn't the one I'd chosen. My quilt was supposed to be stitched by Aunties in that hut. *Haole* Aunties offering safety and love through the power of creativity.

Wasn't it made just for me? So much for the meaning I had imagined. Or maybe the meaning was never in the stitches themselves.

The room—this sanctuary I built—wasn't what I thought. But then again, neither was the life I had planned. That doesn't mean it isn't significant.

I love this room. The white linen curtains look out onto a pond filled with wildlife and a neighborhood of ice skaters. The blue wallpaper with palm trees and pineapples. Queen Anne furniture. Grass-woven rugs. The refinished—did it myself—rocking chair I used to nurse my babies. And finishing it off with a pillow decorated in a matching *honu*—a gift from my only daughter.

Before I could even use this room for myself, Kai came home from living abroad. He planned to build his own computer using parts that might not match or fit.

This time, not decorating the room with LEGO projects, but with computer parts.

It turns out that mismatched pieces can still build something.

Chapter 25
Yom Kippur—A Day of Atonement

Three lawyers.

Two judges.

Five years.

Countless trips between the mainland and *Hawai'i*.

One deposition—five hours; two hundred and four pages—where My Father could no longer hide or deny.

The truth spilled out: he'd plotted my abuse before I was born and carried on until I stood over him with a baseball bat in hand.

The court ordered a settlement.

Meanwhile, his third wife—the mail-order one, Gucci Girl—was all over Facebook. She was flaunting her new Gucci bags and dishes—who knew?—and posing next to her red Porsche. Proof enough for me, he wasn't broke; he was just hiding the money, placing it all in his wife's name.

And that house? The one I grew up in and once wanted to own—or maybe burn down? He 'sold' it to a friend, who flipped it straight to the Gucci Girl.

My first high-profile lawyer dropped the case and handed it off to a junior associate. I don't think he ever believed my story—even with a certificate of merit and a PTSD diagnosis attached. The new lawyer didn't do much either, except for one important thing: he took a deposition. I already knew the house money wouldn't hurt My Father financially.

My Father wanted to pay me a million dollars under the table. A million? If that doesn't spell guilty, I don't know what does.

I refused.

Now the junior lawyer just wanted to get his cut and run.

No public court testimony.

The only record of admissions? A deposition document filed in a cabinet. The lawyer pushed hard for the first sum offered.

I'd done my homework.

I researched what other survivors who had been awarded settlements in the state had received. These were students abused by school authorities—not by their own parents. Those parents still stood behind their children. The settlements were triple what I was being offered. As if being abused by a parent was less damaging.

We need to be patient.

The lawyer didn't care.

Like the *Honu*.

My lawyer threatened me, "Settle, or I'll sue you. And you'll get nothing." The lawyer would sue ME?

No trial.

No public reckoning.

We SETTLED.

My Father kept finding excuses not to pay. Months went on and on. The judge finally set a payment deadline. Ten percent interest per day on any unpaid balance. The deadline was September 30th.

Unbeknownst to the *Hawai'ian* judge, that date fell on the holiest day in the Jewish calendar. Yom Kippur. The Day of Atonement.

My Father had never been religious—not once—unless it was convenient. Come to think of it, maybe a lot of people are that way. Remember that part about him being half Jewish? Well, now it was convenient. He'd never practiced Judaism, unless you count not being accepted into the Naval Academy because of a Jewish last name.

That, apparently, made him devout enough. Suddenly, Yom Kippur was his 'high holy day.' Therefore, untouchable.

The judge wasn't buying it. That was the deadline. September 30th.

By sundown, the check had cleared.
He paid.
On Yom Kippur.
The Day of Atonement.

Karma?
Providence?
Call it what you will but, to me, it tasted like justice.

I immediately called the Royal Hawaiian Heritage Jewelry shop—the one on King Street, across from the State Capitol and the Palace. *Hawai'ian* jewelry lore stretches back to the 19th century. According to legend, Queen *Kapi'olani* and Princess *Lili'uokalani* received engraved bracelets at Queen Victoria's Golden Jubilee in 1887, and *Lili'uokalani* commissioned designs dating back to 1862.

I needed a reminder that this was real.
There had been atonement.
On Yom Kippur.

I ordered a bracelet, gold with black-enameled letters spelling *K A L A H A L A*, the *Hawai'ian* word for atonement. I had looked it up online. I asked the jeweler to engrave, "Yom Kippur 2018" inside the bracelet. The man on the phone paused. "Are you sure that's the word you want?" he asked. He told me he was Jewish, and something about the way he asked made me pause.

Later, I would think it might have been a little divine intervention.

"Yes," I said. Absolutely yes.

I began writing this book—which by the way started as *Decorating with LEGOS*, turned into *Broken Pieces*, and eventually negotiated to *Piece by Piece*. Double-checking my facts—like a good author should—I looked the word up again. This time, the internet translated *kalahala* not just as 'to atone,' but also as 'forgiveness.'

Forgiveness?
Can I forgive?

The bracelet stays on my right wrist, just below the *honu 'tattoo'*—unless the beeper goes off walking through TSA. It must want to announce to the world the atonement AND forgiveness it represents. I wear it while writing, cooking, playing the piano, swimming, and dreaming.

I still look at it.
Still feel it.
I needed atonement.
I got it.

Forgiveness?
That's a question I'll let sit for now.

Chapter 26
Keys to Healing

When the courtroom and greedy lawyer failed me, I turned to the one thing that I could always depend on—music.

I've said it before—music saved me. Not once. Not metaphorically. Over and over again, in ways I'm still discovering. It gave my sick, trauma-wired body something to push back with—dopamine, endorphins, rhythm. It gave me something to do with the feelings I wasn't allowed to have. Music gave me proof that I could work, focus, and express myself. It taught me not only how to survive, but thrive.

A world-renowned forensic psychologist once diagnosed me with severe PTSD after a five-minute conversation. We didn't talk about trauma—just about my life. He didn't ask about the pillow, or the bat, or the dark. But somehow, it was all still there in the way I answered the mundane questions.

I remember it all, and it's not sunshine and roses. That's the difference between me and so many other survivors. I didn't forget. I didn't dissociate. I remember.

Do you hear me, Honolulu Assistant District Attorney? Always testifying that no one remembers?

Somehow, I managed anyway—at least most of the time. Husband. Family. Friends. Education. House. Career. Decorating. Gardening. Shopping. Cat. Dog. Bearded dragon.

MUSIC.

In my 'favorites' photo folder, there's a black and white picture of me at my mother's spinet piano—not yet two years old—eyes fixed, possessed, already claimed by something bigger than me.

My mother had dreams of being a music major. Instead, she sang at church and styled herself like Jackie Kennedy. I was her project, too. The pretty daughter in homemade, tailored dresses, seen but not heard—though not for lack of trying. She provided 'affordable'—what I call cheap—lessons in everything: dance, voice, *hula*, embroidery, piano. Strangely enough, not reading, math, or science—all classes I could have used a boost in. As a child, I thought it was about money. As an adult, I believe she simply didn't want me to outshine her.

I kept practicing my music at home—though by then I had a car and could've just claimed to be 'busy.' My love of music was so strong that I persisted until I had built the skills I needed, one by one. Always trying out, rarely making it, but never giving up. Like everything else, I figured it out.

Music became a place.
Not a task.
Not a role.
A place I could be.

Not to perform.
Not to impress.
Just exist.

In *Hawai'i*, music is part of life. You don't just listen. You live it. I remember *hula* lessons, *Tiny Bubbles*, the sound of slack key guitar, and Queen *Lili'uokalani's* song *Aloha 'Oe*. That music made sense of things that didn't.

I didn't perform music to please others—not my mother, not my teachers, not even God. I played for myself. I sang to survive. I still performed—but not for the reasons all those around me assumed.

My parents promised me a piano—any piano I wanted—*if* I graduated from university—like I wasn't going to make that work. I needed a piano of my own. I would no longer live in their house—a fact obvious to anyone who cared to look. Of course, they lied.

I bought a decent upright. During the first move, the movers took a big chunk out of the front. But that was nothing compared to my mother's piano—its keys were chipped by my little brother pounding on them with a toy rifle.

My upright wasn't the grand piano I dreamed of. Not the one I had earned. It was the one that would let me teach, that would make me money. That was the real reason. They never invested in my music—they commodified it. Still, I held the dream.

Over the years, I visited piano stores and played all types and sizes—Steinways, Yamahas, Schimmels. None of them spoke to me, like the *Honu* in the ocean or the ancestors.

After my husband and I put four children through college—well, three graduated and one majored in Life 101, but we helped with a house for his budding family—I'd tell him, "I played a beautiful piano today at the store, and I would love to buy the grand I've always wanted." My Husband responded, "Then you'll need a new husband." I didn't want a new husband—I wanted a new piano.

My journey for atonement was never about money. It was about setting the record straight—for the survivors who hadn't yet spoken, for the truth that had been buried too long.

I wanted My Father to answer for what he'd done. I wanted to deter other pedophiles by proving there could be judgment, and there could be penance.

But My Father wasn't ashamed. He wasn't embarrassed. He had settled. Quietly. Without apology. Without pain. He would never acknowledge the suffering and the pain, and he certainly would not acknowledge healing. I had to do that myself.

To ease pain and suffering—a settlement's purpose—I used part of the money in a way I hoped would bring healing.

A dear friend who owned a piano store knew my story and, for over thirty years, understood my need for a special piano that reflected who I'd become. He knew it wasn't about music alone. He knew exactly what it would mean.

On a Sunday, when the store was usually closed, he unlocked the door and showed me a Bösendorfer. Seven feet, matte black, whisper-soft touch, one string per pitch. A piano that responds to emotion, not force. It didn't have the extra keys—inside info for pianists—but it costs just as much.

Then he quietly went outside to 'work' in the flower beds. I touched her keys and began to play. She answered me as if she was speaking—like the ancient *Honu*—saying, "It will be OK."

My friend delivered the piano himself, along with a massive bouquet of roses. The piano was carefully moved to a spot that offered privacy, but where it could also be showcased.

One Friday night, as I played and only my Husband was around, he said, "You know, it's great to be married to a musician. I always get to listen to beautiful music." He had acknowledged the contribution music made to my life in his own way.

I didn't get justice.
Not really.

I did get music.

And that was the largest brick I could add to the life I've been building.

Chapter 27
The Sound of Silence

Funny thing about harmony—it sounds beautiful until someone decides who's allowed to sing.

State Vocal Music Association: The name alone sounds official enough to belong in the capital, maybe with a shiny state seal embossed on the letterhead. Parents and students assume it's a state agency—an organization built to protect and elevate the arts. But it isn't. It's a private nonprofit. Which means it can do whatever it wants while convincing the rest of the state it speaks for all of us.

For years, I believed in it. I admired the CEO—her confidence, her knowledge, the way she commanded a room. I thought she was everything a strong woman in music education should be. I attended every workshop, every conference, every festival. I followed the rules. I believed in the mission: to educate, inspire, and elevate vocal music. What I didn't realize then was that this organization wasn't built on harmony. It was built on control. And the unspoken rule was simple: fall in line or get out of tune.

When I first took over as a district manager of the organization, it was a disaster. After paying outstanding bills, the district was four thousand dollars in the red. I received a box out of a minivan that was as disorganized as the LEGO boxes in my closet. Students were crying after events, not celebrating. The experiences weren't educational or inspiring—just exhausting.

I did what I always do. I got to work. Inside the box I was gifted was a small portable computer that had seen better days. I was told it was broken and to throw it away. Lucky for me, my husband is an IT guy and did miracles—whoo-hoo.

It didn't take long to see what had happened. There was a single spreadsheet, and the numbers did not add up. My hypervigilant brain remembered when the district president explained that the money had been deposited into the treasurer's personal bank account because it was "just easier" Easier? Sure. Illegal, possibly.

By the end of my third year, the books were clean, every receipt was accounted for, and there were sixteen thousand in the bank. Young singers and directors were smiling again. Teachers came to meetings. We even had real meals—with dessert—at bi-annual meetings. It wasn't glamorous, but it was honest. It finally felt like we were back in tune. Then Micah died.

A week later, when I could barely breathe, I received an email and a phone call from the 'president' of the organization. Mind you, it wasn't a condolence note. Not a simple, "We're thinking of you. It must be hard for your students. What can we do for them?"

He demanded a meeting—at the same festival where I was taking my grieving students. I asked for a little more time. A place where I was not giving all my attention to my students. They had just lost one of their beloved teachers to suicide. Let's just add I might need a minute to breathe.

Instead, a letter came from a lawyer. Demanding my resignation as district manager. Ordering that the bank account be turned over—to the same people I'd once suspected of skimming off the top. It warned that if I didn't step down immediately, I'd be banned from judging, holding office, or ever being recognized again.

Banned even before they told me what I'd supposedly done wrong. Or shared exactly what drew such ire?

The accusations shifted as fast as their stories. First, I had cheated at the Choral Festival. Next, I'd embezzled money. Sure. With sixteen thousand dollars sitting in the bank? They changed their minds over and over while gossiping lies behind my back.

Let's be real—I did stand up for someone. A past president who'd been forced out for health issues. I believed—like most of the non-governing membership—that we'd voted him in by a majority vote. Apparently not. Turns out, the vote was only for show. Somewhere along the way, a new constitution had been written stating that the board appointed positions, and the membership's vote was merely 'advisory.' Making up quiet rules? Why not.

I refused to turn the money over to the one person I knew was complicit in the lost money and had changed my scores at the festival to look like I had cheated. Curious?

They couldn't fire me—I was a volunteer. Now it was time they made sure I disappeared. No judging. No meetings. Blatant lies spread like butter on bread. Well—more like the way my husband spreads it. He doesn't spread it; he lathers it.

But true to form, I didn't disappear. I kept showing up. I kept taking my students to festivals, standing in the same rooms as the people who'd told lies. They'd smile those tight, polite, passive-aggressive smiles, then turn and talk about me the moment I walked away. Oh, there was that one time we walked into the association's sight-reading room, and the judge said, "Chamber Choir, like in Gas Chambers." Not cool, especially with Holocaust survivors' grandchildren in the room. My students sang their hearts out anyway. They shared their music.

Years passed. Other opportunities came: Shoa Requiem with PBS; Detroit Pistons basketball games; shows with the voice of the Detroit Red Wings, Karen Newman; Rockefeller Center; state capitols; Carnegie Hall—three times—and many more.

The old vocal association CEO retired, and a new one replaced her after a long interview process. Most directors were surprised, but he was musical as well as calm, fair, and logical. A rare combination for a music director, especially in the vocal arts. It didn't happen overnight, but eventually the 'state' office began to see what had really gone on and to respect the work I did with students and music. They began to understand that the two-inch file they kept on me was mostly fiction. Slowly, things started to shift.

One day I was asked to fill out the qualification form to adjudicate Musical Theater Solo/Ensemble. With former students on Broadway and in Hollywood, I had more successful alumni than anyone else in the organization. I was qualified over and above. I soon received an email inviting me to judge. I was elated. Maybe I would finally be recognized for the work I had done. I got to judge and, besides the first student—who didn't follow the rules and number the measures—every other teacher and student walked away feeling educated, inspired, and positive about their experience. Isn't that what we always said we wanted?

For a moment, it felt like things were finally shifting. Like the work spoke louder than the rumors. A few months later, I was honored with an Emeritus Lifetime Achievement Award.

At the ceremony, the old CEO sat in the back row, arms crossed, her entourage around her in case she fainted or felt weak. Her smile, tight enough to crack glass. When my name was called, I stood at my seat. Years before, award winners walked to the podium and gave short speeches. This time? No speech. No walk across the stage. I accepted a small glass orb etched with Emeritus: Sheryl Hauk. The other winners were upset, but I was simply grateful to be recognized at all. It wasn't much—a token, really— but it shimmered in my hands like proof that truth sometimes takes the long way home.

When the ceremony ended, one of the office secretaries came up to me. She placed her hand gently on my shoulder and whispered, "Please know you are not the only one she goes after. She came after me too." This soft-spoken, competent, logical, and kind woman standing before me? I've often wondered what rule she didn't obey.

Not long after, the new CEO—the one who'd begun to clean up the mess—sent a short resignation letter. No reason. No real explanation. Just gone. And soon after, a new CEO stepped in. Hard to follow, right? For me, not at all. I know this pattern.

I contacted members of the committee that had chosen him. They all responded that they would not talk about it. I was told the new CEO was part of the 'inner circle.' Strange—he had never been a choral director, but now he was going to lead choir directors.

Just like that, the music stopped again. No invitations. No judging. No acknowledgment. Silence. But not the peaceful kind. This was the kind of silence that hums just beneath the surface—the kind that fills a choir room after a song ends and the air still vibrates. The kind that lets you know the sound is gone, but the echo isn't finished yet.

For a long time, that silence made me ache. I'd given everything—time, talent, energy, love—and it took one vindictive voice to undo it. It's strange how quickly truth can be buried under bureaucracy. But over time, I realized something that changed everything: institutions don't get the final say. They can take your titles, your access, your invitations. But they can't take what you've built in the hearts of students.

Music doesn't live in bylaws or budgets. It lives in memory—in the sound of a student's laughter between warmups, in the tears of a senior who finally believes her voice matters. In every moment someone chooses to keep singing even when the system tries to silence them.

Yes, they froze me out again. But I am not stopping. I will keep mentoring, conducting, and creating spaces where music still means something real.

Funny thing about harmony—it can't exist without dissonance. And I've learned to love the dissonance, because it's honest. It tells you when something's wrong. It demands to be resolved.

They can keep their silence.
I'll keep my song.

Chapter 28
Breaking the Silence

Everyone has to join some kind of club at least once—a book club, a sewing circle, a wine night. It's practically required—somewhere between a rite of passage and community service.

I've done my time. Once, I was in a group called Stitch and Bitch. Not quite technically a book club, yet it served many of the same purposes. While we stitched, we bitched: about our jobs, our husbands, our kids, the PTA, the patriarchy. We made little Xs in different colors—pictures to hang on the wall or sew into throw pillows. It was therapy, just with needles.

Other book clubs I participated in were similar—less about books, more about bonding over life's injustices. But one stands out: the neighborhood book club.

We started as strangers. Before long, our circle settled into a core: me, from *Hawai'i*; a professor of economics from Iran; a nurse from the Eastside; an automotive executive of Indian heritage; a pharmaceutical saleswoman; a Forbes-ranked VP; and a mom with two small boys, still learning her way forward.

We were Catholic, Lutheran, Protestant, Hindu, Muslim, Jewish, and atheist. We debated novels and shared ideas. We drank wine—don't all book clubs?

I was the oldest—not always the wisest—but definitely the most seasoned. With my Leo energy and Year of the Tiger status, I may have—occasionally—dominated the conversation. Yet, for years, we created a safe space for different perspectives, for big conversations that tried to change the world—at least our small suburban world.

The monthly hostess, with the mostest, had the critical task of choosing our next book, and each event was filled with decorations, the newest hors d'oeuvres, and a variety of wines—planned and expertly prepared with creativity and flair. We read and bantered through *The Red Tent*, *The Biography of George W. Bush*, *The Glass Castle,* and *The Kite Runner*—all bringing different perspectives together and leaving us laughing and looking forward to our next meeting.

This went on for years as our children grew, our careers blossomed, and we became closer and closer. We knew each other's secrets, and a genuine bond existed. Then we read *Never Let Me Go*. This novel explores the lives of clone children raised in a seemingly idyllic but ultimately dystopian setting, where their purpose was organ donation and eventual 'completion.'

I got triggered. No big surprise to you or me, but the book club?

At the time, I was beginning to find my voice and had started the legal battle against My Father. We had had differing opinions before, but this time I was triggered—over the top. The hostess shared that if her child needed an organ, she would do ANYTHING—even if that meant using a clone child. The whole table agreed. There was no discussion; all the members would protect their own above all else—except me.

I reminded them that was what the majority of the people in Europe did during the Holocaust—remember how much I loved to read about that as a child? Add to that the truth I knew too well; the adults in my childhood had done the same thing—they stayed silent. They protected themselves and their children.

No one sitting at that book club table budged. No one even wanted to discuss it. That was that. My alarm went off. I could not understand why my book club friends would not fight for ALL the children, clone children included. Wasn't that what I was doing? Putting my safe and comfortable space aside to save children and other survivors? Was there ever really a choice? I could stand up for all the children with my voice, or I could sit down and stay quiet.

I chose to stand up.

It wasn't easy. It meant stepping out of my comfort zone, risking friendships, and facing uncomfortable truths. But silence was no longer an option. The children—every child—needed to be protected, and their stories deserved to be heard.

That moment marked the beginning of a journey from words to action—one that would lead me to testify in legislative hearings, fight for justice, and use my voice to make a difference.

Chapter 29
Close my Eyes and Jump

Here I was, suing My Father while diving headfirst into legislative advocacy, trying to rewrite laws for survivors of childhood sexual abuse. I didn't have time—especially emotional time—for book club wine nights and polite disagreements about fiction. I was in the thicket trying to hack my way through. I admit I badly missed all the late-night friendship talks, backyard BBQs, and girls' nights. But I realized sometimes you trade one thing for another.

What I didn't see right away was that the sacrifice wasn't just time or friendship—it was comfort. The deeper I got into my own case, the more I realized this wasn't just about justice for me. The silence was bigger than my story. The system was built to outlast us. So, I stopped waiting for someone else to fix it. I did what I could, with what I had, where it mattered.

Let's be very clear. I believed that if I filed a lawsuit, won my case, and made a good enough argument, the lawmakers would do the obvious right thing—protect children and allow justice for adult survivors. Cut and dried, right?

NOT A CHANCE.

Let's break it down, statistically. In the U.S., one in seven girls and one in ten boys are sexually abused. It's called a 'silent crime' because most victims don't tell. Non-offending adults often ignore the signs. Abusers are usually trusted adults who manipulate situations and hide in plain sight. The effects aren't always physical. They're behavioral. Emotional. Invisible. Misread as 'moody' or 'difficult.' Children are often blamed.

Stunning numbers.

That's what really made me step forward. Leave my comfortable book club. It was what I had to do. I didn't know how. I was just figuring it out as I went.

I wasn't an activist or a lobbyist. I was just a mother, a wife, a teacher, with no real choice—driven by something deeper than myself. And there was a lifetime of unspoken memories. I'd survived by improvising—no plan, just instinct.

Jump.
Adjust.
Land.
Repeat.

My human rights lawyer—the one on that business card who took his cut—gave me the name of a friend who is a brilliant legislator, Linda Ichiyama, in the State of *Hawai'i*. The two had met in law school. I emailed her expecting no response.

Once again, I closed my eyes and jumped.

Representative Ichiyama emailed back extremely quickly—not a regularly occurring phenomenon in politics, or education, come to think of it.

She'd just had her first baby but agreed to meet me at her office anyway. When I arrived after searching through the labyrinth of rooms, the newborn baby lay swaddled in her arms. Her mother was there to help—love the *Hawai'i 'Ohana* way of support for new moms. This brilliant young woman took the time to sit with me and listen to my story. She valued what I had to say. That doesn't mean she agreed with everything. Smart people don't just agree. Yet, she listened.

I remember telling her something My Father had claimed—over and over—that *Hawai'i* had an extraordinary number of adult-child 'relationships,' the kind no sane person would accept as okay. She was shocked. At first, she didn't believe me. Yet, she didn't dismiss me.

She sent me to another representative. I told my story again. Then another. Then another. I laid the groundwork. No roadmap. No organization backing me. No backdoor agenda. Just a singular survivor trying to be the voice for those who couldn't speak.

I flew back to: children, hockey practice, choir performances, doctor appointments, mowing the lawn. You get the idea—the everyday challenges moms juggle. It was nice that Representative Ichiyama had the support of her mom and family. I didn't.

Back on the mainland, I signed up for legislative notifications, combed through bills, and tracked committee calendars. Just your average book club commitment, right?

Soon I discovered a new bill was being introduced to extend the statute of limitations for child sex abuse survivors. And guess whose name was on it? Yep—the young Linda Ichiyama with a new baby.

I didn't *have* to get involved. I'd already had my day in court. But others hadn't. Others weren't ready to use their voices or face their abusers. Something deep down inside, in my core, told me it had to be me. If others couldn't use their voices, I would use mine. What was I thinking? No one gave me the 'OK' or a manual. I was on my own. AGAIN.

I took time off from teaching school—which I rarely did, since no substitute really wants to follow lesson plans for four choir classes and AP Music Theory. I flew the ten hours to *Hawai'i* —without corporate or lobbyist funding. Paid for, ironically, by My Father. Lovingly referred to now as the 'atonement settlement.' Or, more accurately, 'blood money.'

I was going to testify at a committee meeting and make them agree with me. We would right the wrongs, bring accountability and atonement. This time, I literally closed my eyes and figuratively jumped into a hotbed of lava.

I sent personalized emails to every committee member. I'm sure they loved me for that, or not.

I donned my mainland-size 8 best dress, heels, of course. In hindsight, I probably should've stuck with *aloha* wear and flip-flops. I headed to the Capitol with no idea where to go or how it would all work.

I passed the metal detector test and went to a committee room. It had a long table for legislators and their aides, as well as four rows of chairs for the public and press. Not as impressive as my mind had imagined. I listened to testimony on bills I didn't understand or had never heard about for an hour.

Inadvertently, I sat next to the Assistant District Attorney who would testify against 'my bill.' Oddly enough, there was a little lady with bright purple hair who had something to say about almost every single bill. Amazing. She certainly used her voice. I didn't know then that we'd become friends or that I would come to see her as a mentor.

Finally, after hearings on companion dogs, handgun regulations, and mental health initiatives, the bill I'd been waiting for came up on the agenda—a bill to extend the statute of limitations window for survivors of childhood sexual abuse. This was a duplicate of the law I had used in my quest for atonement.

No brainer. Or so I thought.

The Assistant District Attorney—next to me—got up first. She announced the Attorney General's office did not support the extension of litigation for sexual abuse of minors. She went on to state, "Victims don't remember. They're not reliable." Victims? You mean survivors. Right? She completed her testimony by adding that too many plaintiffs lied about their abuse.

What?

I remember.

I am a *kupuna* and I REMEMBER!

Why would anyone put themselves through years of lawyers, questions, and blame to bring a lawsuit? Did I mention that the law requires a forensic examination of the survivor and a special certificate of merit that validates the *victim's* story?

It was hypervigilance mode for me. I could feel the cortisol rushing through my body, hands shaking, stomach ready to vomit, and head screaming,

"I REMEMBER EVERYTHING!" Every last horrifying detail relived, over and over, like a movie in my head, every day.

Finally, the man behind the computer monitor called out, "Anyone else here to testify on this bill?" "I am," I said, raising my shaking hand quickly. I didn't have a coach, a mentor, or even a friendly nudge, so I hadn't signed up to testify. At that point, I didn't have a clue how the whole process worked.

Why was I shaking? I'd conducted three hundred students at once. Could it be the PTSD? The cortisol? Or the five gifted neurological conditions?

The man behind the computer waved me forward. "Two minutes," he said. I slowly walked to the seat that he gestured to. The room was packed. Standing room only. Survivors, supporters, even a few seeing-eye dogs. You could feel the anticipation tickling just beneath the surface.

And yet... the long committee table in front of me was mostly empty—at least when it came to legislators. Quietly, some of them stood and slipped out the side doors when my bill was called. Not all—but enough that I noticed. Did anyone else notice? Must have been the hypervigilance.

Two minutes—the clerk emphasized again. Now, even my voice was shaking. Two minutes to tell the truth of a lifetime.

I'm not even sure what I said. Something about justice. About children. About memory. I do remember turning around to face the Assistant District Attorney, saying rather shakily and loudly, "I'm over 50, and I remember.

My body remembers.
My life remembers.

And I am still living with the consequences of things I never asked for."

When my two minutes were up, Cynthia Thielen, a *kupuna* legislator, with gray hair and comforting eyes—and years of using her voice for the people—looked at me gently and asked, "You said you came from Michigan. Isn't that where the Nassar case is happening? Can you tell me more?"

She opened the door. She was listening. She wanted to understand. She wanted others in that room to listen and understand. That moment—the eye contact, the pause, the quiet question—was the start.

They heard my voice.

Where is justice?
Where is atonement?
Where is the accountability?

I REMEMBER.

Everything else after that is kind of a blur. I met other advocates. I met the press. I met the woman with the purple hair. That bill extending the window was eventually passed into law. That window gave over 800 voices the opportunity to speak out and find justice in the courts. Over one hundred priests in *Hawai'i* were served the day after the governor let it pass without signing it into law.

The victory was short-lived.
The window was only for four years.
And those four years?
They went fast.

I wasn't done yet.

Chapter 30
Let My Voice Be Heard

I think—no, I am convinced—that laws like the ones I testified for could—would—deter pedophiles. Maybe not all, but some.

Pedophiles often operate knowing their victims will stay silent—until it's too late to prosecute. Whether you're eighteen or a hundred, justice shouldn't expire just because trauma kept you quiet.

So I kept going.
I fought.
Except when I didn't.

Suddenly, things got harder. Bills vanished in political wrangling, stuck in the House Chair's office, or lost in a 'special committee.'

Then COVID hit, and everything shifted. Testifying in person wasn't an option anymore. Meetings moved online, making it harder to connect, harder to be heard. Experts warned that the rate of abuse in homes would multiply with the stress of quarantine.

Sometimes, the press assumed the legislation had passed bills into law. Instead, they quietly disappeared. Or a powerful special committee chairman changed the effective date, bumping it seventy-five years into the future—that's not a typo.

Politicians didn't just hide in the Capitol—they even hid in TSA lines. Once, I flew back to *Hawai'i* just before Christmas, desperate to breathe again after a school shooting back home—close to where I taught. Can you believe I was just a little triggered?

Hawai'i.
Music.
Ocean.
Survival.

As I stood in the TSA PreCheck line, emotionally exhausted and waiting to return to the mainland, I heard a voice behind a mask and recognized it from the first time I had ever testified. See? I do remember. I quickly turned around to the voice.

"Are you…?" "Yes," she answered. "I know your voice. I'm the survivor who testifies from the mainland on sexual abuse of minors."

I could only see her eyes because of the mandatory COVID mask. She blinked and asked, "Oh! Didn't your bill pass?" No, it didn't, lady! You'd think the committee vice chair would know that. You'd be wrong. Or she knew—and just didn't care.

For ten years, I wrote emails, testified in person, showed up on Zoom during COVID, pounded on office doors, visited the Capitol basement press room. I even camped out two full days in a key legislator's office, only to watch her slip out the back. The aides didn't know what to do with me. But Representative Thielen did. The *kupuna* legislator was so impressed by my tenacity that she showed up at that office herself, standing there in solidarity while the aides squirmed like eels out of water. She was badass.

Once, I traveled 4,000 miles—lots of Delta points—walked into a Senate committee hearing to testify, and the judiciary chair said, "We're out of time."

Out of time? I stood up anyway and said, "I came this far—I will be heard." The chair was stunned. I was a Leo, after all. I testified.

Compromise—that's what we so often do as we build. Sometimes the pieces you thought would work don't. Sometimes someone knocks the whole project down, and you have to start over. And over and over. Alone. With no organization behind my name. No press release. No campaign. I did not have a hidden agenda nor was I trying to be famous. I simply wanted survivors to be heard and taken care of—all of them. Even the ones I hadn't met or who hadn't found their voices yet.

Near retirement, I took my students to my home in *Hawai'i*—one last journey together before I stepped away from their journeys. My gift to them.

I planned the trip—every last detail—without the help of a company. I took nineteen students, one colleague, and a rotating cast of family members to my home on *O'ahu*. I would have taken all of my students, but some had their cruises and posh vacations 'already planned.' Either that or they didn't want to learn six new songs and spend any extra time with me. To be honest, the ones who signed up thought it was just a spring break trip. Beach, sunshine, and maybe some singing.

I had different plans.

We arrived at my childhood home, and their first stop—after food and sleep—was a place where it's impossible not to feel small, yet also tethered to something vast and eternal. The *Pali* doesn't just welcome visitors—it claims them, if only for a moment.

This sacred cliff was where *Kamehameha* united the islands under one king, ending centuries of needless wars. As my students gazed across the *Ko'olau* mountain range, the wind rushing around them like a living spirit, they did the only thing that made sense.

They lifted their voices in song.

And in that moment, they began to understand the power of *Hawai'i*.

From there, we traveled by bus to the farthest destination from our hotel, to learn about the rich cultures of Polynesia at the Polynesian Cultural Center—stopping one more time for roadside *huli huli* chicken.

Once again, the students were asked to sing, filling the room with *Aloha*. "Bravo sensei," said the friendly workers, bowing deeply in appreciation.

The students sang on the USS Missouri, looking out at the Arizona Memorial—the same place My Father once took me on a skiff, pretending reverence. They swam in the ocean, ate on the shores of Pearl Harbor, and visited the *Hawai'i* State Capitol.

I had written ahead and asked permission for my students to sing in the open Capitol rotunda—symbolizing the sea, sky, and open society of *Hawai'i*. I learned that in fourth-grade social studies.

The young, now seasoned, representative's aide replied, a little suspiciously, "What's your agenda?" If I'm being honest, I had a secret wish. I just wanted my students' beautiful voices to rise out through the rotunda, and offer something holy to the spirits of survivors. That's not what I told the aide—I know how to play the game. We were approved to sing.

Representative Ichiyama herself met us and we were invited into the House chamber. The *koa*-paneled room was empty, except for me, my students, and my friend with the purple hair. Then the Representative, a law graduate of George Washington University, shared the meaning of *kuleana*—civic responsibility—the effects of global warming on *Hawai'i*, and the importance of education. Then my students sang—just for her—in that beautiful, acoustic space.

Wearing t-shirts that read *"Let My Voice Be Heard,"* the students lifted their voices and sang *Earth Song*—Frank Ticheli's hauntingly beautiful anthem, which has always felt like the soundtrack to my story.

> *Sing, Be, Live, See.*
> *This dark stormy hour,*
> *The wind, it stirs.*
> *The scorched earth*
> *cries out in vain:*
> *O war and power,*
> *you blind and blur,*
> *the torn heart*
> *cries out in pain.*
> *But music and singing*
> *have been my refuge,*
> *and music and singing*
> *shall be my light.*
> *A light of song*
> *shining strong: Alleluia!*
> *Through darkness, pain, and strife,*
> *I'll sing, be, live, see…*
> *Peace.*

The sound swirled through the chamber like smoke through a broken wall. Tears came to Linda's eyes, and mine too. It was a moment I can't describe.

We moved into the rotunda. Aides, legislators, tourists, and staff lined five stories of open-air hallways, leaning over balconies as the music rose. When the last note hung in the air, a woman approached me.

"I remember you," she said. "I was an aide to Representative Thielen. I remember the day you testified using the Nassar case as an example." Her boss, the badass *kupuna*—all soft eyes and gray hair—had retired during the years of this long fight, but not before helping to pass that first bill into law.

The woman leaned closer and said, "There's a hearing happening upstairs right now—the newest version of your bill. You should go."

I never get children involved in my cause. I never shared my story with them—or even with my own children until they were adults. I had five students older than eighteen on that trip, ready to graduate and step into the world. I drew them close, told them why we were really at the Capitol, and invited them upstairs. They went quietly, respectfully—up the back staircase in their matching choir shirts.

Let My Voice Be Heard.

They sat silently while I testified. And they saw me. Truly. For the first time, they saw me.

That bill did pass into law—but not without compromise. It extended the statute of limitations, but only moving forward. No retroactive justice would be provided for anyone abused before August 2024. If your trauma happened before then? Too late. If you're over 60? Still too late. As if memory has a shelf life or justice an expiration date.

I am over 60. So is my sister—the one who never had justice. Never found her voice.

I found my voice.
Because I remember.
We remember.

The brilliant Representative Ichiyama—the one who'd met me years earlier with her newborn on her hip—now with two school-age children—graciously invited me to the governor's bill signing.

As I waited to enter the press room for the signing of the bill, Rep. Ichiyama introduced me to officials from organizations across the state who'd 'supported' the bill. They hugged and congratulated each other—though I don't remember seeing any of them testify.

Finally, we were all shuffled to the beautifully decorated *Hawai'i* Governor's press room. Rep. Ichiyama had saved a special seat for me. I had waited years for this moment. I found the seat with my name on it, sat quietly, and the ceremony began. And then, to my horror, my Apple Watch started to *beep*.

Seriously? Comic timing at its worst. I froze, horrified, cortisol flooding through my already hypervigilant body. It was a reality check. From that moment, I might as well have been invisible. No interview, quote, or front-page photo. The law wasn't reported like the others signed that day.

But my goal was never fame. My goal was to be heard, and make sure survivors' voices carried further than mine. To make sure predators knew: the silence was breaking.

Hawai'i will always be imprinted on who I am. To everyone else in that room, I was just the woman who lives on the mainland. Except I'm not from the mainland. This is what I wanted to say, loud and clear,

"Mahalo Hawai'i—for a start. But this cannot be the end. It is your *kuleana*, your responsibility, to take care of the survivors, even those from the past."

After a speech by an official from an organization—for the cameras—the governor signed the bill. I was able to thank him, and he asked why I was there.

I quietly answered, "I am a survivor."

"I'm sorry," replied Governor Josh Green, M.D., before pulling me in for a final picture.

As all the VIPs vanished, I was invited back to Representative Ichiyama's office. "You were right." She said as we sat down in her office. "Right about what?" I asked.

"About what your father told you about *Hawai'i* and children. We launched Operation *Keiki*. When we bust pedophile rings, the police report that no one's afraid. They just act like nothing's going to happen to them."

Because they believe nothing will.
And most of the time—they're right.

But I'm still here.
Still testifying.
Still building.
Still showing up.
Still writing.

This project?
It's not finished.

And now—finally.
My voice will be heard.

Chapter 31
All That Jazz

Hawai'i has its signature music—slack key guitar, ukulele, soaring falsetto, and those warm, rich alto tones that live deep in your chest. I still have the stack of Cecilio & Kapono and Kalapana records to prove it. The music raised me. Emotionally, spiritually, and through improvisation.

I named one of my sons Kapono for his middle name because his voice stuck with me so deeply. That's the kind of impact his music has on me and who I am.

Music of *Hawai'i* isn't so different from jazz. Both are rooted in place. Both are shaped by suffering and joy. Both are complex enough to let you feel everything at once. Improvisation, extended harmonies, and chord progressions—from the AP Music Theory teacher who can't stop analyzing everything.

No one ever exposed me to jazz as a child—not the vocal kind, not the big band kind, not the messy, brilliant kind born right here in America. Not even at Baylor. Waco Hall echoed with Bach, Brahms, and every European master imaginable—but no *Hawai'ian* music. And certainly no jazz. What a shame.

I was grateful to Baylor that let me sing Handel's *Messiah* and meet John Rutter.

What music did I choose for my cassette player? Always the sounds of home. Homegrown *Hawai'ian* sounds.

During spring break of my third year at the university, I was fortunate to tour with the Baylor University a Cappella Choir.

That tour took me places I'd never been—Texarkana, Natchez, and New Orleans. The old New Orleans, before Katrina.

We ate beignets—those deep-fried, powdered-sugar bombs—and sipped café au lait. We saw women of the night stumbling out of alleyways, which seemed to shock some of the other students. Not me. I'd transferred city buses on Hotel Street—Honolulu's red-light district—when I was eleven. I had my education.

I wandered the French Quarter, and that's when I found it. Preservation Hall. A small room. No microphones. People standing shoulder-to-shoulder, sweating and swaying. And the music—alive, unrepeatable, sacred. Jazz. Real jazz. The kind you feel more than hear.

For the first time since I'd left home, I watched musicians close their eyes and jump—improvising purely for the moment. This was music that spoke to the insides of my soul.

I could've stayed in that small, cramped room forever. But eventually, the bus was leaving for our next stop. I ran back—still carrying it with me—knowing something spiritual had just happened. Something that would change me—I just didn't know what to do with it yet.

Years later, I became the choir director at a large suburban high school. Our feeder school director had studied with—and gone to school alongside—internationally recognized jazz educators and composers. She taught, recorded, and composed vocal jazz herself. And she was a middle school teacher? Go figure. Teaching what I lovingly call "The Beasts." She's definitely earned her angel wings. Her students expected me to teach jazz because she did.

Me?

Teach jazz?

I'd heard it once—at Preservation Hall. I could teach Brahms, Handel, and John Williams without blinking. But jazz? That was another world.

Still, that didn't stop me. I'm a Leo. A survivor. Music had saved me more than once. So I did what I always do. Once again I closed my eyes and jumped. I fumbled. I learned. I asked for help. I grew as a director—and my students grew as performers.

Over the years, they sang jazz at the Disney Jazz Celebration, the Gold Company Invitational, and the Rochelle Vocal Jazz Festival. My ensemble was named the state organization's top jazz ensemble three years in a row—and top specialty choir two years in a row. I only applied these years—no money, no resources, no support.

The vocal jazz ensemble's first big invitation came from the New York Vocal Jazz Festival, directed by Dr. Steve Zegree. The guest clinician? The legendary Greg Jasperse—yes, the one I cheered for like a teenager at a Beatles concert. Did we go? Of course, we did.

And what did we sing? *Voice Dance*. Our feeder school director told us that Greg Jasperse had initially written it for a friend's wedding. At the time, it was the most complex piece my students had ever sung—though in the years that followed, they'd master even tougher ones.

We drove to New York City in a giant snowstorm and nearly didn't make it. Our bus driver snapped the windshield wiper off. Really? I'm a choir director on a mission, so I made him drive to the nearest repair shop in the strange suburbs of Cleveland and get it fixed. Then off we went again.

We finally made it to a small studio for our promised clinic with the composer of *Voice Dance* himself. Greg did not disappoint. He was gracious, brilliant, and everything I'd hoped for.

He inspired us—me, I'm a groupie—so much that three years later, I once again dragged my students halfway across the country to the Disney Vocal Jazz Festival—just to experience Greg Jasperse again. I was just as starstruck the second time. Which says a lot coming from someone who was raised with John McCain, had a cousin who worked for Joe Biden, and grew up on *Oahu* parallel to Barack Obama—we called him Barry.

The years started to fly by. My former students were now composing, performing, and recording professionally. My children had flown the coop—and I had welcomed grandchildren. Greg Jasperse eventually took over the vocal jazz program that his teacher had started at Western Michigan University. He wanted to shape students with music every day, not just at festivals.

Together with the New York Voices, he launched a vocal jazz camp—teaching, mentoring, and healing through music. Not the kind of healing handed down by courts or committees. The kind you build yourself—from sound, from story, from whatever scraps you're left holding.

Let's talk about blood money. My definition? Atonement for what was done to me as a child. And let's be true—no amount of money can ever undo that. What happened changed everything. But blood money can still do good. It can still be applied in ways that make a real difference in people's lives, especially in the lives of kids who need music to survive—just like I did.

I put that settlement toward causes I believe in—efforts to change statute of limitations laws, local resources for survivors, and a podcast called *It Shouldn't Hurt to be a Child*.

Eventually, I wanted to give directly to kids. With the help of Greg—now my true friend, still a groupie—we created a scholarship. I named it after the first piece I ever taught by Greg Jasperse: *Voice Dance*. The Voice Dance Scholarship.

Just one more way to make something out of what My Father tried to destroy. The best part? My Husband's company matched every dollar. Each year, two students—not just one—receive that gift. Two students. Two voices. Two new lives reshaped by music.

That's what healing can do.
That's what atonement—reimagined—can become.

And the giving didn't stop there. CARE House of Pontiac partnered with Suite Dreams to create bedroom makeovers for child survivors—safe, comforting spaces where they could finally rest without fear. Rooms rebuilt and redecorated piece by piece, turning pain into color, light, and belonging. That instinct—to make a space feel safe again—has always been my kind of healing. And that, too, came from the same "blood money."

My Father is furious that his settlement money helped fund such initiatives as a podcast called *It Shouldn't Hurt to be a Child*—and a scholarship for singing.

This new project?
It can't stop.

Blood money set the stage; jazz brought the atonement, and healing found its rhythm.

Chapter 32
My Wish

I used to think wishes were for candles and stars. Now I know they're something else. Quiet things we keep locked inside—until we're ready to say them out loud.

As a child:

I wished I didn't have to eat bananas until they were coming out of my ears.

I wished I didn't have to taste Dove soap.

I wished I didn't have to stop piano practice because my mother *needed* me to get her tea.

I wished my pets hadn't 'disappeared.'

I wished I wasn't made to walk on prickly grass to take a picture I didn't understand.

I wished I could sleep without fear.

I wished I didn't have to sit in the bathroom alone in pain while the rest of the class learned something new.

I wished I could truly tell my best friend who I am.

I wished I could keep my head up in school.

I wished I dreamed of what I might be.

I wished God heard my pleas.

I wished My Father fought the monsters, instead of being one.

I wished someone had listened.

Stopped the abuse.
Stopped the hurt.
Stopped the silence.

And let me be a kid.

As a young adult, wife, and mother:

I wished I would have swung that bat sooner.

I wished I had saved my siblings.

I wished Kai didn't have a tumor the size of a softball in his skull.

I wished my son and grandchildren never learned the word migraine from me.

I wished I didn't have to carry five neurological conditions.

I wished I wasn't triggered by 'bad behavior.'

I wished I could have been a wife and mother without so many demons.

Now:

I wish I could see the water every morning from my bedroom window.

I wish I had a pool in my backyard to swim in the water every day.

I wish the spiders would make their web anywhere besides my fire-pit.

I wish hiking up an Italian hilltop wasn't a struggle when my mother ran it at eighty-seven.

I wish the giraffe lady would stop gossiping and 'bumping' me in dance class.

I wish I could work where there is always respect and professionalism.

I wish not to feel alone in a crowded room.

I wish not to be pitied or called damaged.

I wish someone would hold me and kiss me—not because I asked, not because I earned it.

I wish I could truly be the voice for the silent.

I wish every survivor knew this: what happened to you does NOT define you.

Not the silence.
Not the screaming.
Not the bruises, or the soap, or the shadow at the door.
You don't have to forgive to be free.
You don't have to explain to be believed.
You don't have to be fixed to be whole.

I wish every child who learned to walk on eggshells—or prickly grass—could walk freely now.

I wish every adult still carrying their child-self in pieces could find peace in their skin.

I wish you knew: what happened to you is NOT who you are.

I still wish. Not with candles. Not with stars.
Wishes don't raise children.
Wishes don't testify at the Capitol.
Wishes don't teach harmony to a roomful of grieving students.
Wishes don't sit beside your brother in a courtroom.
Wishes don't build swimming pools or decorate hospice rooms.
Survivors do.
We do.
With whatever we have left.
With what we're given.
With what we drag out of the dark.

Even if the pieces don't match.

Even if some are missing.

Even if we step barefoot on them in the middle of the night.

I still wish.
But I also build.
I also fight.
I also stay.

Because someone might be watching. Because someone might be whispering. Because someone else might still be trying to find their first piece.

So if I get one more wish…

I wish they knew:

They are NOT alone.

That we all stand together—survivors, advocates, allies—united in the fight against the injustice inflicted on our most defenseless.

That we demand accountability from those entrusted to protect us, yet who too often betray that sacred trust.

This is not just outrage. It is beyond outrageous. It is a call for truth, for justice, and for a future where no child suffers in silence.

May we build that future piece by piece, together.

Chapter 33
Decorating with LEGOS

Kai was eight years old when he got sick. We didn't know how bad it was at first. Just a tonsillectomy, they said. Routine.

I sat in the waiting room with a folder of graduation invitations, sending out news of my daughter's academic achievements, while my third child was supposed to be getting his tonsils removed.

Then came the little room. And you already know what I say about that—never trust the little room.

A doctor white as a sheet. Not from anesthesia. Not from a scheduling delay. From fear. Kai had a skull tumor. Everything changed in that moment. Three hospitals. Teams of specialists. Twenty-one hours of surgery. Nine pints of blood. Seven days in the ICU. A son—nine years old—clutching his giant stuffed orca in his arms, brave in a way no child should ever have to be.

What I remember most, strangely, is the LEGO building blocks. Not the blood. Not the tubes. Not even the diagnosis. Just the click of small plastic bricks on a tray table while he healed.

In between the scans, the wires, and the terrifying quiet of machines that hummed more than beeped, Kai built.

Piece by piece.
Set after set.

Tiny hands assembling tiny bricks into entire worlds. Castles. Starships. Cities. Dreams. He built elaborate airplanes and whole fleets of ships from Star Wars, including the Millennium

Falcon—all from LEGO kits that gave him something to control when everything else felt broken.

I didn't sit with him.
I didn't build.
I just watched—as the bricks piled up at the top of the stairs, right outside our bedroom doors. That's where he built his worlds.

That's where I pretended not to fall apart. And, somewhere in the middle of the trauma, I realized that's what I'd been doing my whole life.
Taking broken pieces, mismatched colors, parts from different sets, missing instructions, and building something anyway.
Making it hold.
Making it mine.

Kai still has a tumor on his carotid artery. He knows it's there. He chooses not to address it. That's his decision now—one I have to respect, even if I don't understand it. Because he's grown, he's whole, in his own way. He gets to decide what healing looks like for him.
I know the building bricks helped. The quiet ritual of creating something—anything—when the world felt like it was falling apart. It wasn't just a distraction. It was survival. It was the first piece in building a life that could still hold.

For him.
For me.

Before the surgery, there was fear. So much fear. Not just mine. Kai's, too. His dad's. The kind that doesn't show up in medical charts or family updates.

My mother-in-law once told a story, something she remembered clearly after one of her hospital stays, when the haze lifted for a moment. She recalled, "The day Kai was going in for surgery, he was belligerent. He didn't want to go. He fought with his father and refused to get in the car. His father kept trying to explain—but it didn't matter. 'Why, why, no, no,' Kai cried. Finally, his father just looked him in the eye and said, 'Because, it's to save your life.'" That's when Kai got quiet. Just—quiet.

I've never asked Kai or my husband what went through their heads that day. Maybe I should.

Kai was healing. The family was healing that summer after his surgeries. It was time to clean up. My husband had built two rows of shelves in Kai's room to display his models. Each one had a story. I decided it was time to wipe off the dust—to start cleaning. I lifted the Millennium Falcon carefully to dust underneath. I wasn't careful enough. The large ship built with hundreds of brick pieces slipped from my hands and crashed to the floor.

My mind screamed, "How could you do this? How could you do this to your child?" To this little boy, who had already been through so much.

Horrified, I turned toward the door.

There stood Kai.

He didn't look upset.

He looked at me—really looked at me—and said, **"That's OK, Mommy. We can just build something new."**

Epilogue
Still Building

That was the moment. Not in the courtroom. Not in the hospital. Not in the choir room or the governor's office. It was there, in the hallway of a child's room—when I thought I'd ruined something sacred. When Kai looked at me and said: *"That's OK, Mommy. We can just build something new."*

That's the whole book, really.

We decorate with what we have; hand-me-downs and junk-sale finds, memory and metaphor, broken pieces. We build from the cracked, mismatched, scattered pieces—not perfect, but ours. Sometimes, whole enough to carry us forward.

I've lived long enough to know healing isn't a destination. It's a rhythm. A process. A pattern you return to—like breath, like music. You don't have to revisit the worst days to prove you survived them.

You did.
I did.
I'm still here.

Not because everything is fixed. Not because I forgot. But because I learned to build something stronger—with boundaries, with chosen family, with love. With humor—let's not forget that. Dark humor is a survival skill. If you can't laugh while standing in line at TSA in a post-legislation depressive episode, you're missing out.

I keep showing up for:
Family
Friends
Students
Alumni
Choir members
Survivors

The younger me who once whispered, "Help!" into rooms full of people who didn't listen. Now I get to be the one who hears.

If you're reading this and you're a survivor:
You are not alone.
You are not broken.
You are not too late.

If no one believes you, believe yourself. If they looked away, look inward. You'll find the truth. If you're ready to tell your story, do it in your own time, your own voice, your own way. If you ever drop the Millennium Falcon? You're not alone. You can build something new, too.

I even found a way to turn part of my story into action. I helped produce a podcast called *It Shouldn't Hurt to be a Child*— while Karen Newman, a dear friend, narrates the story of survivors speaking their truth about childhood trauma and what real accountability can look like.

I support organizations like Child USA, where legal research and advocacy help create stronger protections for survivors, especially those of us who remembered too late for the courts, but right on time for ourselves.

CARE House of Pontiac later partnered with Suite Dreams—a project that gives child survivors new bedrooms so they don't have to sleep where the hurt happened. Some of that same blood money helped make that possible. I didn't pick paint colors or curtains, but knowing those rooms were being rebuilt felt like its own kind of healing. Maybe that's the best kind of decorating there is—turning what was meant to destroy into something that helps someone sleep safely again.

> We may not be able to rebuild what was stolen.
> We can build something better.
> A little off-center.
> A little cracked.
> But strong, and beautiful, and absolutely ours.

> I'm not done.
> Neither are you.

Resources

If you need support, here are
a few places that listen:

National Children's Alliance
www.nationalchildrensalliance.org/cac-coverage-maps
Dedicated to making Children's Advocacy Center (CAC)
services available to every child in the country.

RAINN (Rape, Abuse & Incest National Network)
1-800-656-HOPE (4673) or rainn.org
Confidential 24/7 hotline and online chat for survivors of sexual
violence.

Darkness to Light (Preventing Child Sexual Abuse)
d2l.org
Education and prevention programs aimed at ending child sexual
abuse.

National Suicide Prevention Lifeline (U.S.)
Dial **988** for immediate, confidential support.

Childhelp National Child Abuse Hotline (U.S.)
1-800-4-A-CHILD (1-800-422-4453) or childhelphotline.org
Free, confidential support in over 170 languages for children and
adults.

Child USA (Advocating for Legal Reform and Survivors' Rights)
childusa.org
Legal research and advocacy for survivors of child sexual abuse and neglect.

It Shouldn't Hurt to be a Child Podcast
(CARE House of Oakland County)
carehouse.org/podcast
Real stories and education about preventing child abuse and supporting survivors.
U.S. and Canada

Child Welfare Information Gateway (U.S.)
childwelfare.gov/state-child-abuse-and-neglect-reporting-numbers
State-by-state child abuse reporting numbers and family support services.

International and Global Resources

Canadian Centre for Child Protection
protectchildren.ca
National programs addressing child safety, online exploitation, and survivor advocacy.

British Columbia Helpline for Children
1-800-663-9122 or gov.bc.ca/gov/content/safety/public-safety/protecting-children/reporting-child-abuse
24/7 provincial reporting for child abuse or neglect.

Ontario Children's Aid Society
ontario.ca/page/report-child-abuse-and-neglect
Resources for reporting and preventing child abuse within Ontario.

Child Helpline International
childhelplineinternational.org
Connects to hotlines in more than 140 countries; many
European nations use 116 111 as their helpline number.

UNICEF Child Protection
unicef.org/child-protection
Global programs protecting children from violence, exploitation,
and trafficking.

Global Survivors Fund (GSF)
globalsurvivorsfund.org
Supports survivors of sexual violence worldwide through
reparations and advocacy.

INHOPE
inhope.org
International network of 57 hotlines working to remove child
sexual abuse material online.

NO MORE Global Directory
nomoredirectory.org
Worldwide directory of sexual and domestic violence helplines
and shelters by country.

The Survivors Trust (U.K.)
thesurvivorstrust.org
Umbrella organization offering free, confidential support to
survivors of sexual abuse across the U.K.

Kids Alive International
kidsalive.org
Provides safe housing, education, and advocacy for children in
crisis globally.

For Adult Survivors

Adult Survivors of Child Abuse (ASCA / NAASCA)
ascasupport.org
Peer-led support model for adults recovering from childhood abuse of any kind.

National Sexual Violence Resource Center (NSVRC)
nsvrc.org/survivors
Evidence-based information and survivor-centered guidance on healing and trauma.

Enough Abuse Campaign – Survivor Support
enoughabuse.org/get-help/survivor-support
Resources for adults who experienced childhood sexual abuse, including education and recovery tools.

Pandora's Project
pandys.org
Online community and educational resources for adult survivors of sexual assault and abuse.

International Trauma Center
internationaltraumacenter.com
Trauma-informed global network offering education and healing resources for survivors.

International Society for Traumatic Stress Studies (ISTSS)
istss.org
Professional and survivor-oriented organization sharing research and best practices in trauma recovery.

Acknowledgments

This book did not come into being on its own. It was built, like the rest of my life, from the voices, hands, and hearts of many people who stood beside me.

First, my deepest gratitude to Eric and Bobbie, whose insight, editing, and persistence helped shape these pages into their truest form. I know I pushed you—with endless edits, demanding timelines, and what you kindly named 'Sherisms.' Thank you for rolling with all of it, for your patience, and for reminding me that this book was worth the work. You managed to shape my words without taking away my voice, and that is a rare gift. For that, and for your good humor along the way, I am endlessly grateful. And I promise not to send new chapters or send any more yellow edits… probably.

To my students of forty years—our journey taught me as much as I ever taught you. Even if you thought I was too tough or didn't always make the choices you wanted, know that I cherished every moment. Every rehearsal, every performance, every conversation shaped me. I always took us down the paths I believed were best for you, and I remain deeply proud of the music and memories we built together.

To my book club friends, who filled the years with wine, stories, laughter, and truth—thank you for reminding me that healing and wisdom often grow in the spaces between friendship and honesty.

To my friends, especially those who read drafts even when it was hard, who offered feedback, and who wrote endorsements to stand beside me—you gave me courage when I needed it most. Thank you for not stepping back or pretending I hadn't written this but, instead, for seeing me and telling me to keep telling my story. So many others just walked away.

To Becky and Donna—my steadfast friends of fifty and forty years—thank you for walking with me through decades of laughter, loss, and rebuilding. You encouraged me even when I wanted to quit—both this book and, at times, life itself. When I doubted myself, you reminded me of who I was. When I was ready to stop, you told me to keep going. Your belief in me has been a lifeline, and your friendship will always be part of the foundation I stand on.

To all the strong, thoughtful women who have stood beside me through this journey—the ones who showed me what courage looks like in action. To Representative Linda Ichiyama, former Representative Cynthia Thielen, and advocate Carolyn Golojuch—the lady with the purple hair who has been my steadfast advocate in *Hawai'i* since the first time I testified—thank you for showing me what strength, intelligence, determination, compassion, integrity, courage, resilience, grace, wisdom, empathy, and conviction look like when they come together in one voice. You've each taught me so much.

To my grandchildren—thank you for Metallica, for hiking, for laughter, and for the light you bring into my days. You are my joy. I hope to leave you not only memories, but empowerment and a legacy that reminds you to keep building.

To my children and to their partners, I know how hard this is for you. I know it may be embarrassing or difficult to have pieces of our story on these pages. But I had to write, and I had to share. Thank you for allowing me the space to tell the truth, even when it was not easy.

To my husband—thank you for the moments of encouragement along the way and for sharing in the journey that brought me here. You didn't know what you were getting into, but it has certainly been an adventure. Truly.

Because of friends and family like these, I am able to pass this book forward.

And finally, to every survivor who finds pieces of their own story in mine: this book is for you. May you know that your voice matters, that your challenges do not define you, and that you are never alone. The pieces of your story—no matter how scattered, sharp, or mismatched—can still be gathered. They can be rebuilt into something strong, something meaningful, something that belongs to you. It may not look perfect, but it can still be beautiful. We can build again.

About the Author

Sheryl Hauk grew up in *Hawai'i*, a *haole* shaped by a culture that taught her resilience, belonging, and the power of music and *'ohana* (family). Her life unfolded in parallel with Barack Obama's in Honolulu—both shaped by the island's rhythms, its unspoken expectations, and the ocean that grounds and humbles. Those early lessons in balance,  identity, and empathy became the foundation for a lifetime spent building connection through music and storytelling.

Sheryl dedicated more than forty years to music education, serving as a conductor, clinician, and Fine Arts Coordinator while mentoring thousands of students who found their voice under her direction. Many have gone on to national stages and professional careers in music, theater, and the arts, including actress and singer Ryan Destiny, composer and conductor Christian Kolo, vocalist Chelsea Helm, and Broadway actor Danny Kornfeld.

Her choirs have performed across the United States—from concert halls and jazz festivals to national ceremonies and state events—and her work as a music educator has been honored for its innovation and excellence. Sheryl has received the MSVMA Lifetime Achievement Award, been named a Grammy Teacher of the Year Quarterfinalist, and was recognized as a Life Changer of the Year nominee. She has also served as an adjudicator and guest conductor for state and national music organizations, helping shape the next generation of music educators and performers.

Beyond the podium, Sheryl is a survivor and an advocate for justice. She produced the podcast *It Shouldn't Hurt to be a Child* and has testified before legislators to help change statutes of limitations for survivors of childhood sexual abuse. Her commitment to using her voice for change—whether in the classroom, the courtroom, or the community—has made her an enduring advocate for those learning to speak their truth.

In *Piece by Piece*, her debut memoir, Sheryl brings that same honesty, dark humor, and hard-won resilience to the page, revealing how music, creativity, and courage can rebuild even the most fractured lives.

Sheryl lives with her husband and, together, they raised four children. Today, she treasures time with her four grandchildren, who live just a short drive away, reminding her daily that joy, purpose, and love can always be rebuilt—sometimes from the very pieces we once thought were broken.

sherylhauk.com

Feedback

If this book helped you in any way, please consider leaving a review on Amazon. Your opinion may help others realize they are not alone and help them rebuild.

Share your feedback, stories, or insights here:
https://sherylhauk.com/feedback